Dunstan Thompson

on the life and work
of a lost american master

Dunstan Thompson

on the life and work
of a lost american master

D. A. POWELL & KEVIN PRUFER, EDITORS

The Unsung Masters Series at Pleiades Press
Warrensburg, Missouri, 2010

ISBN 978-0-9641454-1-2

Published by Pleiades Press
Department of English & Philosophy
The University of Central Missouri
Warrensburg, Missouri 64093
&
Department of English
Winthrop University
Rock Hill, South Carolina 29733

Distributed by Small Press Distribution (SPD)

Cover Image of Dunstan Thompson © by Philip Trower
Book design by Kevin Prufer.

2 4 6 8 9 7 5 3 1
First Pleiades Press Printing, 2010

Financial Assistance for this project has been provided by
the Missouri Arts Council, a state agency, and the
National Endowment for the Arts.

Contents

An Introduction

If you were a young poet in New York in the early
1940s, you'd likely have heard of Dunstan Thompson.
Maybe you'd even have met him, or noticed him from
across the room drinking a dry martini at a cocktail party, a
slim, voluble man in his twenties with a narrow face and
heavy eyelids, quick-witted and sharp, observant of the
mannerisms and affectations of others. The war in Europe
dominated the headlines, and Dunstan was working on a
book of poems and editing a small poetry magazine, jok-
ing wryly about his near future reading manuscript submis-
sions in Camp Dix.

His close friend Howard R. Turner writes in a letter that
he never understood why Dunstan left Harvard before the
end of his senior year, though he suggests that he had seri-
ous disappointments with the English Department.* His
longtime friend Philip Trower, however, says he dropped out

---

* For all background information, I have relied primarily on personal corre-
spondence with friends of Dunstan Thompson and, less frequently, on mate-
rial on the poet published during his lifetime. Much of this will soon be avail-
able in the new Dunstan Thompson archives at the Huntington Library.

to avoid an inevitable academic expulsion. Problems or not, Dunstan appears to have treasured his time at the university, especially the attentions of three poets on the faculty, Robert Davis, Theodore Spencer, and especially Robert Hillyer, about whom he had especially fond memories.

But on arriving in New York, it didn't take long before Dunstan was well known in the literary life of the city and friends with many of its most prominent literary types, including Horace Gregory, Marya Zaturenska, George Barker and the eminent anthologist Oscar Williams. His friend Howard Turner would later describe him as "quite a marvel—friendly, very funny, somewhat overwhelming in manner, even dictatorial at times." Others would point out that he was hyper-sensitive, highly strung, dazzling, and impractical, quickly endearing himself to the older generation of editors, writers, and socialites.

Himself a bit of an outsider—he grew up in Annapolis and Washington, D.C., his father, Terry Brewster Thompson, a naval officer of New England origin, his mother descended from an old Maryland family, both fervent Catholics—Dunstan had always been curious about the lives and manners of the rich. Philip Trower recalls a story he would tell years later of meeting one of New York's "top millionaires" and noticing that, though immaculately dressed, his evening pumps were scuffed and worn. For Dunstan, Trower says, "it was like meeting Augustus and noticing a stain on his toga…. I can imagine him going over the incident later as he lay in bed…was it indifference, lack of respect for his hosts, or a small rich man's economy?"

He was making news as editor of *Vice Versa*, a short-lived, lively literary magazine he started with his friend Harry Brown. With a youthful teeth-gnashing, the twenty-two-year-old Thompson wrote in its first issue, "this magazine shall be a means to attack the smugness, the sterility, the death-in-life which disgrace the literary journals of

America." And, in dozens of reviews, Dunstan, Harry, and their friends doled out luke-warm praise to John Berryman ("quite competent when it comes to writing four and five stress iambic lines") and Eudora Welty ("worth reading"), or condemned W. C. Williams (a "tiresome fake"), and Louis MacNeice (a "clever fraud"). *Vice Versa* growled at potential contributors, threatening to "carefully burn" any poems that arrived without a self-addressed stamped envelope. It nipped at the heels of the literary lights of the day. In a short essay, it attacked *Poetry* magazine, which it characterized as "very much like Hamlet's father. It is dead, and yet it walks..."; when *Poetry*'s venerable editor was roused to anger, the experience was "like having a dead maiden aunt stand up in her coffin and do a jig.... Go back and lie down, maiden aunt. You wouldn't want someone to drive a stake through your heart, would you?"

But for all Dunstan and Harry's editorial outspokenness (and they did, now and then, dole out praise to the likes of Wallace Stevens, John Betjeman, and Randall Jarrell), their slim magazine printed some of the finest poetry of the age, including work by Ezra Pound, Edith Sitwell, Conrad Aiken, W. H. Auden, Weldon Kees, Dylan Thomas, and the very young Howard Nemerov (who later during the war would rescue Dunstan from a bar fight in London). Dunstan funded *Vice Versa* himself with a legacy left to him in 1934 by his great aunt Leita, the widow of a former Chief Justice. And then, after three issues, it folded. The magazine was just too costly to run and Dunstan was no businessman. Still, the legacy was enough to make him a "man of independent means" from the age of sixteen to his death forty years later.

But this is jumping ahead. In 1942, shortly after the demise of *Vice Versa*, he was headed to Europe and the war. Poorly adapted to military life (his wartime acquaintance Edward Field described him as a curiosity to the other enlisted men), he failed at officer training camp. Instead, he found himself assigned to the Bureau of War Information in London as a GI, and later as a Corporal in the Air Force. (In 1959, he'd write of his achieving the Good Conduct Medal over the objections of his superiors, summarizing his war experience thus: "I had a gallant war record—carrying Coca-Cola bottles to sergeants and writing the Colonel's letters to his friends back home. He used to mess up the grammar afterwards to make them sound authentic.")

He was, however, clearly making light of his experiences, creating for friends years later a cartoon image of a bumbling, comically ill-suited intellectual lost in the American Armed Forces. The truth, apparent in his poems and what can be gleaned from the memories of his friends, is more complex. In London, he witnessed the worst of the bombing of the city and must have been in constant contact with those returning from, or heading to, the fighting on the Continent. Whether or not he considered himself fit to fight, he had a lively, sensitive mind, one quickly attuned to the peril on both sides of the English Channel. His poems of this period reflect little of the clownishness with which he amused his friends; instead, they are fraught with violence, anxiety, and, often, despair.

The memories of his friend Howard R. Turner, who often saw him in London, hardly resemble Dunstan's recollection of his own ineptitude. "His humor and wit could never be blasted by any bombardment," Turner writes. "And whereas I trembled visibly at the sound of approaching flying bombs, one of Hitler's nastiest so-called 'V for Vengeance' weapons, Dunstan, embodiment of cool courage, reacted with appalled amazement one night at my suggestion that we leave the comfort of a friend's electric heater and hide downstairs in a basement shelter. I never saw him afraid of anything or anyone."

Nevertheless, Dunstan had time during the war to read a great deal and to become acquainted with the best literary people in the city. In a letter to Conrad Aiken, T. S. Eliot describes him as getting to know "all the right people there in two seconds flat"—the Sitwells, the Spenders, Cyril Connolly, and others.

Still, his longtime companion Philip Trower notes, "Dunstan was no social climber. Even if he had wanted to be, it would have been unnecessary. He was so interesting and out-of-the-ordinary that each new friend and acquaintance would introduce him to others. 'Haven't you met him? Oh, you must.' For many people, he was that sort of person."

In romance and friendship, Dunstan was a figure of some discussion. Edward Field, who discovered the "homosexual underground" in the armed forces toward the end of the war, describes him as affecting the mannerisms of the aesthete, doing nothing to hide the fact that he was gay. And only a very literal-minded reader would fail to see the overt homoeroticism of many of the poems he wrote during this time, desire balanced against intricate, violent, longing imagery of wounded boys, vanished boys, furtive boys, boys in hospitals, boys "blown to ribbons" on battlefields.

Philip Trower describes him from a different perspective, distinguishing between the deep, unabashed friendship he felt for his many male peers to whom he dedicated his poems, and his private search for physical union. During his early years, he writes that "there seems to have been no lasting or stable relationship.... He seems to have sought that kind of love outside his circle of friends."

In 1943, Dunstan's first poetry collection, *Poems*, was published to unusually prominent reviews. The influential *Tomorrow* magazine called it "The book of the season" (though the review itself was lukewarm and Dunstan himself noted in pencil on my copy, "Really, this man is too illiterate"). Other reviewers were more generous, if a little perplexed. *The Commonweal* would compare him favorably to Rupert Brooke, proclaiming "here is a living, speaking voice of youth enmeshed in war." *Poetry* magazine (despite his earlier jabs at the editor) would praise his rare concision, the beauty of his imagery, his technical dexterity, finally proclaiming, "Dunstan Thompson deserves the appellation *poet.*" *The Nation* declared him the author of "some very bad poetry… self indulgent and full of private symbols." But that, the reviewer H. P. Lazarus suggests, was almost beside the point, for "the violence of his vision of the inner world, compounded of war, death, incertitude, isolation, reflects the cataclysm which traditional modes of thought and feeling are undergoing in the world today." Meanwhile, *The Partisan Review* cited his "dash and splendor" and the dour *Times Literary Supplement* shook its head at Dunstan's "selfish egotism," his excesses of imagery and adornment.

Lament for the Sleepwalker, his second book, received similar attention, establishing Dunstan Thompson as one of the most talked about young poets of the age, a poet Edward Field would describe as one of the "stars of modern poetry," not far behind Hart Crane, Auden, Spender, and Dylan Thomas in Field's youthful estimation. Philip Trower describes the poet around the time of this book's publication back in New York, living at the Algonquin Hotel, still in his twenties, but already a "figure" on the American poetry scene. The future for Dunstan Thompson seemed very bright. If you were a struggling young poet at the time, he would have been an object of envy.

Shortly thereafter, the publisher Dodd Mead financed a journey to the Middle East, which resulted in a travel book, *The Phoenix in the Desert*, to be followed later by the novel *The Dove with the Bough of Olive*. The English publisher Secker & Warburg put out a volume of selected poems. Meanwhile, Dunstan had settled with Philip Trower in the village of Cley next to the sea in England.

Then, as far as the general public was concerned, Dunstan Thompson disappeared.

In July 2005, the poet Kolt Beringer bought a worn-out copy of Dunstan Thompson's now-forgotten *Lament for the Sleepwalker* at a used bookstore in Minneapolis. He'd never heard of the poet. Neither had his professor, D. A. (Doug) Powell, who photocopied a few pages, then called me on the phone to read them to me. They were, we agreed, extraordinary, metrically complex, imagistically fantastic, surreal, and startling. I remember telling Doug that the work reminded me of some odd blend of Edith Sitwell's exuberant, violent image-making and Rupert Brooke's deep sadness. For Doug, the poems were evocative of Hart Crane.

I bought a copy for $2.50 from an on-line seller, and Doug and I spoke frequently on the phone about the poems, about Thompson's intricate rhythms, the odd convergences of eroticism and violence, heartbreak and chaos. There was, we agreed, something gratuitously flamboyant about these poems, the metaphors very nearly overwrought, Thompson's rhythmic line so often veering from contemplation into ecstasy or fits of anxiety or despair. (And then, every now and then, he'd slip in a line so plain-spoken and abrupt as to throw all the moodiness off balance. At the end of the first "Song of the Soldier," the entire complex grammar of the poem collapses terrifyingly into the final phrase "A war means this.")

Here, we decided, was the WWII poet that literary history had failed to bring us—a poet weirdly attuned to the war even as he made of it moments of complex, even baroque, beauty and sexuality. Here was a soldier who finds in the war not mere futility or valor, but desire, sensuality, and a kind of horror that is both deeply personal and all-encompassing.

But who was he? We'd never heard of him. None of our friends had heard of him. No one, it seemed, had any idea who Dunstan Thompson was.

Originally, we thought to convince a publisher to reprint *Lament for the Sleepwalker* and the equally stunning *Poems*, but we could find no rights holder to the work. Thompson's original publisher told us the rights had reverted to the poet decades ago; a brief paragraph on the internet said he'd died in 1975. Doug investigated the files of the *Harvard Monthly*, but could find no clue to where the poet might have gone. We called the heirs to his long-defunct literary agency, but turned up only a card with a long-abandoned address. No family. No executor.

And then, a year later, an internet search uncovered another book, *Dunstan Thompson: Poems 1950-1974*, a thick red hardcover (we'd come to call it *The Red Book* after a while), obviously privately published. But these poems were quite different from those in the first two books. The poet had grown, his interests had changed. Gone were the splendor and eroticism of the early poems, the complexities of rhythm, the eroticism and youthful bravura, to be replaced by a large corpus of verse more rhythmically understated and imagistically calm.

As Philip Trower puts it:

> Both the early and the later poems are the work of the same man. But in the first, it is a bit as though we were hearing the voice of a man running around in a forest fire while in the second it is the voice of the same man after he has reached safety and has had time to reflect on his experiences and the surrounding world in relative tranquility. Or, exaggerating a bit, and using a different image, it is not unlike moving from listening to Stravinsky's *Rite of Spring* to Bach's *48 Preludes and Fugues*.

Also noteworthy is the move from subjectivity to objectivity or the wide range of subjects on which the poet now focuses his aesthetic sensibility. To quote Eliot, it is as though, having found the "still centre of the turning world," it is from this point that he is now able to celebrate its mysteries and sing of its wonders, or launch his darts and javelins at any follies and misdeeds of its inhabitants that attract his attention. Without any rejection of poetic Modernism, there is a re-appropriation and interweaving with it of elements from earlier traditions to the benefit, as I see it, of both.

But this is jumping ahead. In 2004 Philip Trower had still to be found. However, my copy of *The Red Book* acquired over the internet was signed "The author's executor and editor, Philip." It was dated 1986, eleven years after the poet's death. The 1947 *Lament for the Sleepwalker*, I recalled, was dedicated to a Philip Trower. Could this be the same Philip who was now the executor. And was this Philip still alive?

And how could we find this Philip Trower, who, if he were still around, could be well into his eighties? We began with the internet, tracking down the phone numbers of Philip Trowers across the English-speaking world, calling them one by one. Some were amused, others suspicious. None was the Philip Trower we were looking for.

Then, I found a mention of a book on the history of the Catholic Church by a Philip Trower I was pretty sure we'd missed. I called the publisher, was connected from phone to phone, and finally found a young editor who promised to forward my message on to the author. It was a long shot, he admitted; he was pretty sure this Philip Trower was not our man.

A week later, I received an email from Philip Trower, then in his eighties, living in England. "Yes," he wrote, "I am the executor of Dunstan Thompson you are looking for." "The problem is this," he continued, "shortly before his death, he said I was not to give permission for either of the two volumes of his poems published in the 1940s to be reprinted."

Instead of setting our hopes on the earlier books, Philip Trower recommended we look closely at *The Red Book*. Perhaps, he implied, Doug and I might find a project that would include it.

According to Trower, after the war Dunstan tried to find a publisher for his new poems, sending one collection after another to his agent in New York, never with success. A few poems appeared here and there in the late 1940's and early 1950's, in *Botteghe Oscure, The Paris Review, The New Yorker*, but Dunstan Thompson never could reacquire anything like the momentum he had during and shortly after the war. Was it his new subject matter? Or had the literary fashion of the day shifted, leaving him behind? It was perhaps, according to Philip Trower, a bit of both. *The Red Book* includes all the poems written after 1950, ninety-eight percent of them or more hitherto unpublished. He was equally unsuccessful with three novels, several short stories, and a play. Undaunted, he continued writing, reading voraciously, and traveling to London to visit old friends.

Philip Trower describes him after the mid-1960's in deteriorating health, enjoying window shopping in nearby towns, looking at antiques and being taken for drives in the surrounding country.

Dunstan and Philip's relationship was relatively uncomplicated since they had so many of the same tastes and interests and, to some extent, similar backgrounds. From 1945, when they first met, to 1952, they lived together as lovers. But in 1952 both had religious reawakenings. Dunstan, a lapsed Catholic, returned to Catholic practice while six months later Philip, by upbringing an Anglican, joined the Catholic Church, too.

"Dunstan," Philip Trower says, "had had the most intensely Catholic upbringing of anyone I have ever met. By the age of 7 or 8 he was serving the mass of cardinals!" (Trower smartly points out something Doug and I had missed, that "if the early poems should ever be subjected to a sufficiently close analysis, it will be seen that only a lapsed Catholic...could have written them.") So the faith he found after the war was truly a reawakening for him, a return to his beginnings, though with the subtlety, complexity, and strength of an adult.

Of their changed relationship, Trower writes,

> On Dunstan's return from London (after going to confession and being reconciled to the Church at the Jesuit Church in Farm Street) our new way of life began. We had permission to continue sharing the same house, but in keeping with the teaching of the Church, our friendship from now on would be Platonic.... Is it possible for couples with a homosexual orientation to share a house or apartment and live chastely? My answer is Yes, if you do your best to stay close to God through a life of regular prayer. This, I would say, is the *sine que non*.... I often think that had I not had Dunstan to guide me in matters of faith, I would easily have lost my way.

If in his later poems Dunstan Thompson's sensibility shifted from fantastic eroticism, anxiety and grief to a more serene, objective and often joyful outlook on life, one might find in these new poems the same sharp intellect, the same probing curiosity, tempered with age and the erudition that comes with it. Again in the words of Philip Trower,

> Although his return to the Church and the Faith did inevitably change his outlook in significant ways and is responsible for the high caliber and considerable quantity of religious verse in *The Red Book,* the change of content and still more of style and technique had already begun as far back as 1945. As regards the content, there is a new love of and response to the beauties of nature, a fascination with historical personalities and

situations reminiscent of Browning, and a penetrating inter-
est in other people's spiritual and psychological trials and
tribulations rather than his own. All this makes reading *The
Red Book* like a journey of adventure through a new country,
in addition to being, what is more usual on taking up the work
of a hitherto unknown poet, an encounter with a fresh poet-
ic sensibility.

And on reprinting both the later and early poems, Philip
Trower has this to say:

> At the time of his death the poet's great desire was that the
> poems in the *Red Book* should be known and appreciated as
> widely as possibly. However it would have been impossible to
> bring them to the public's attention without a discussion of
> the early poems, too, since it was these which established his
> reputation as a poet. That is why I have allowed poems from
> the two early books to be reprinted here in spite of his hav-
> ing said he did not want those books republished. He said
> nothing about individual poems.

Dunstan Thompson died on January 18, 1975 after a
brief battle with liver cancer. Philip Trower describes vio-
lent winds at his funeral, gusting and turning like small tor-
nadoes. Years later, Trower would suggest that, had the
funeral been somebody else's, Dunstan probably would
have told him, *Someone is furious. He has been defeated.*

For those interested in Dunstan's poetry, the first two
books are, sadly, quite difficult to find. Copies of *Poems*
(both the Simon & Schuster edition and the later Secker &
Warburg edition, which contains a different selection of
poems) surface here and there on the used market, though
Lament for the Sleepwalker has been entirely unavailable for
years. For this volume, we've had to settle for reprinting
only a small folio of Dunstan Thompson's large body of
work. At Philip Trower's request, we've also worked to
provide a balance between the earlier published poems and

the later poems that were collected after his death.

D. A. Powell and I have also brought together here a variety of poets, critics, and old friends in order to suggest something of the cacophony that surrounds the work of this hitherto obscure poet. You'll find little agreement among the essayists about the poems. *The Red Book*, in particular, is the source of differences of opinion.* But that is to be expected, each of these critics making his or her way (often for the very first time) with a writer about whom little of substance has ever been published. In the works from another editor is a volume of Dunstan Thompson's selected poems, which should prove of further interest to readers.

Dunstan Thompson is a vital poet, one unlike any other this country has produced, a brilliant Modernist who underwent a violent and startling change of life and poetic sensibility, one whose work, largely forgotten today, should rank among the best of his generation. Our hope is that this volume might do something to bring him the attention his obvious gifts deserve.

—*Kevin Prufer*
Warrensburg, MO, 2009

---

* Copies of *The Red Book* are currently available for $20.95 through Joseph Pearce at *The Saint Austin Review* Fulfillment Center, 1331 Red Cedar Circle, Fort Collins, CO 80524.

A Folio of Poems

This Loneliness for You Is Like the Wound

This loneliness for you is like the wound
That keeps the soldier patient in his bed,
Smiling to soothe the general on his round
Of visits to the somehow not yet dead;
Who, after he has pinned a cross above
The bullet-bearing heart, when told that this
Is one who held the hill, bends down to give
Folly a diffident embarrassed kiss.
But once that medaled moment passes, O,
Disaster, charging on the fever chart,
Wins the last battle, takes the heights, and he
Succumbs before his reinforcements start.
Yet now, when death is not a metaphor,
Who dares to say that love is like the war?

from *Poems* (1943)

Tarquin

The red-haired robber in the ravished bed
Is doomsday driven, and averts his head,
Turning to spurn the spoiled subjected body,
That, lately lying altar for his ardor,
Uncandled, scandalizes him, afraid he
Has lost his lifetime in a moment's murder:
He is the sinner who is saint instead;
This dark night makes him wish that he were dead.

What daring could not do, the drinks have done:
The limbo lad communicated one
Last sacrament, and, fast as falling, heaven
No longer held a stranger to emotion,
Who, like a star, unsexed, unshamed, unshriven,
Was hurled, a lost world, whirling past damnation:
Circled by chaos but by eros spun,
The devil burned much brighter than the sun.

This bellboy beauty, this flamingo groom,
Who left his nickname soul too little room
For blood on blades of grass, must now turn over,
Feel for the fatal flower, the hothouse sterile
Rose, raised in no god's praise, and, like death, never
Again enjoyed, must make his madness moral:
Washed by the inland waters of the womb,
The salt sheet is his shroud, the bed his tomb.

from *Poems* (1943)

The Point of No Return

See him now, how unhurried he destroys
The tick-tock meaning of the nursery boy's
Nostalgia for love's never-never land,
And, fairy-story prince turned toad, spews out
Not pearls, but girls' garters, when wizard wand
Waves him unwanton, just a Times Square tout:
His smile mints money, but his laugh enjoys
The spoilt child buying back pawn-broken toys.

This all-day sucker for a one-night stand
Gambles his good luck on a steady hand
With queer cards, odd dice, zero numbers, all
Falling by fate too late to lose him health,
Wealth, happiness—gold bricks that build a wall
Around pride's pleasure park with much less stealth
Than rats use, abusing his heart—unmanned
By mother memories more than rats had planned.

Lo, victor, he is vanquished by a small
Miscalculation in a barroom brawl,
Goes for the gutter, makes his getaway
Through sewers, cesspools, urinals, and slums,
Back to the tenement where he can play
His passion to the blandishment of bums:
There, decked with heroin, he has his hall
Of mirrors where no cops can ever call.

What welter of the womb that air breath day
The serpent signified once more in clay:
Later, the data of a Christ-crossed class,
The garbage gift of faith, slag heap of hope,
Concerning charity—the sounding brass:

Those cardinals triple crowned this antipope,
Whose keys are skeleton, whose ring is gay
With fools for jewels, whose blessings playboys pray.

His life—thus, your life, my life—his life has
Its double-feature legends, myths of jazz,
O, Raffles on the roof, O, moon in June,
So, like a blackjack hero, he upsets
The blind queen's balance at the game—but soon,
Too soon, and lovelost by a tune, forgets
His jukebox record plays when X-Men pass:
"The head is human but the eyes are glass."

from *Poems* (1943)

Largo

For William Abrahams

Of those whom I have known, the few and fatal friends,
All were ambiguous, deceitful, not to trust:
But like attracts its like, no doubt; and mirrors must
Be faithful to the image that they see. Light bends
    Only the spectrum in the glass:
    Prime colors are the ones which pass
    The less distorted. Friendship ends
In hatred or in love, ambivalence of lust:
Either, like Hamlet, haunted, doting on the least
Reflection of remorse; or else, like Richard, lost
    In vanity. The frozen hands
    That hold the mirror make demands;
And flexing fingers clutch the vision in a vise.
Each one betrays himself: the ghostly glazer understands
    Why he must work in ice.

All friends are false but you are true: the paradox
Is perfect tense in present time, whose parallel
Extends to meeting point; where, more than friends, we fell
Together on the side of love; where clocks
    And mirrors were reversed to show
    Ourselves as only we could know;
    Where all the doors had secret locks
With double keys; and where the sliding panel, well
Concealed, gave us our exit through the palace wall.
There we have come and gone: twin kings, who roam at will
    Behind the court, behind the backs
    Of consort queens, behind the racks
On which their favorites lie who told them what to do.
For every cupid with a garland round the throne still lacks
    The look I give to you.

The goddess who presided at our birth was first
Of those in fancy clothes fate made us hate to fight:
The Greeks with gifts, good looks, so clever, so polite,
Like lovers quick to charm, disarming, too well versed
    In violence to wear weapons while
    They take a city for a smile.
    By doomed ancestral voices cursed
To wander from the womb, their claws plucked out our sight,
Who nighttime thinking we are followed down the street
By blind end like ourselves, turn round again, and wait,
    Only to hear the steps go past
    Us standing lonely there, at last
Aware how we have failed; are now the Trojan fool
For all the arty Hellenistic tarts in plaster cast:
    The ones who always rule.

We are alone with every sailor lost at sea
Whose drowning is repeated day by day. The sound
Of bells from buoys mourning sunken ships rings round
Us, warning away the launch that journeys you and me
    On last Cytherean trips in spring.
    There the rocks are where sirens sing
    Like nightingales of death. But we,
Hearing excitements, music for the ear, have bound
Our voyage to find its ending where the sterile sand
Spends pearls and coral on a skull. The sailing wind
    Is with us now and then: blows high
    As halcyon clouds across the sky:
Falls fast to doldrums while the moon is also young,
Untided, half to harvest whole. See how our sirens die
    Before their song is sung.

What we have always wanted, never had, the ease,
The fame of athletes, such happy heroes at a game,
Beloved by every likely lad, is not the same
As what we have: these measured methods how to please
    An indolent and doubtful boy,
      Who plays at darts, breaks for a toy
      The sometime valued heart. Why seize
The moment in the garden, on the stair, to blame
Our nameless Eros for his daring? Too little time
Is left for love. When we come back, what welcome home
    Will he award our wounded eyes?
      What uniform be his disguise
In dreams, when sleeping sentries always march away
Once more to war? Now is our novelty: we may surprise
      The faun at end of day.

Make no mistake, my soldier. Listen: bugle calls
Revoke your leisure like a leave, invade your peace
With orders on the run, and, loud as bombs, police
Your life for death. The poet's blood-brick tower falls:
    Even his vanity is gone,
      Which leaves the loser all alone.
      Not private poems, but public brawls
Demand his drumbeat history, the pulse that must increase
Until his heart is ransomed from its jewel. Revise
Your verse. Consider what king's killer did to those
    Who wrote their way between the shells
      That last delusive time. Farewells
Are folly to our serpent queen. She will not sign
Discharge of conscience for a masterpiece, but, hissing, tells
      Failure in every line.
We are the mountaineers who perish on the slopes
Of heaven high and perfect Himalayan peak:

Exhausted by the cold, we can no longer speak
To one another—only signal by the ropes.
　　Those best before us have, alas,
　　Plunged through a gentian-blue crevasse:
　　The snow-blind flaw. Their glacial hopes
Shine as a stream of desperate stars, icebound, and bleak,
That mock their nimbused glory from a frigid lake.
Where we stand now, they stood much farther: climbing like
　　Legendary guides. But traps
　　Were waiting for their last collapse:
Inviting visions from the moon world air—misplace
A step to follow, dance to death. They fell, so we, perhaps,
　　May do as well with grace.

Now noble guests depart for good, wearing our loss
Like flowers. O Damon, decked with asphodel, who moves
Among the shadow dwellers. But he shall hear the hooves
Of unicorns at gallop, see them, coursing, toss
　　Their fluted horns above the cool
　　Unpoisoned waters in love's pool
　　And, kneeling, lay their heads across
A beatific virgin's breast. The day approves
His passage: sunlight on the secret river gives
Bright benediction to his boat. Elysian waves
　　Bear him, the hero, far from us
　　To join the gods. Illustrious!
No words may worship him. The laurel is not all
That withers at the roots, since we, lamenting him, are thus
　　Autumnal for his fall.

Armed, say you? Armed, my lord. So, likewise, you and I,
Who with the butchered ghost must stalk the battlements,
Shall watch—cold-comfort guards—how lonely lie the tents
Where strangers sleep together just before they die.
    Look where their banners in the air
    Are half-staff hung. The cockcrow dare
    Of dawn is mourning in the sky.
Our thoughts like bayonets blood time. What precedents
Of passion shall we use to brave the coward? Once
Bombs are as roses, will he kiss the black-heart prince?
    Honor, more heavy than the sea,
    May overwhelm both you and me
To give no quarter choice at all: gay boys, whom war
Won janizary; youths, who flung away their shields. So we
    Are *mort a Singapore*

Narcissus, doubled in the melting mirror, smiles
To see himself outfaced by tears, and, sorrowing, hands
His ace of love to harlequin of hearts, who stands
The distant edge of laughter. Time's joker still compiles
    Trick score of triumph, trumps the Queen
    To play his knave of emeralds. Green
    Gamester reflects the water guiles
Of palming, reads the gambled cards, and then demands
Another pack to shuffle. But the glass partner bends
The fate five fingers round a saint's stigmata, wounds
    By dealing diamonds from his nails.
    No marveled metaphor avails
To vantage this beloved impersonator twin,
Whose coronet, crown crystal, qualifies a peer. My voice fails.
    In your name poems begin.

from *Poems* (1943)

This Tall Horseman, My Young Man of Mars

This tall horseman, my young man of Mars,
Scatters the gold dust from his hair, and takes
Me to pieces like a gun. The myth forsakes
Him slowly. Almost mortal, he shows the scars
Where medals of honor, cut-steel stars,
Pin death above the heart. But bends, but breaks
In his hand, my love, whose wrecked machinery makes
Time, the inventor, weep through a world of wars.
Guilt like a rust enamels me. I breed
A poison not this murdering youth may dare
In one drop of blood to battle. No delight
Is possible. Only at parting do we need
Each other; together, we are not there
At all. Love, I farewell you out of sight.

from *Lament for the Sleepwalker* (1947)

Songs of the Soldier

I

Soldier, the coward's hero, where
    Is your cocksure courage now?
Death blows the boys to ribbons. They were
    Your friends. Their eyes like lapis glow

With stone-cold brilliants, eyes whose fire
    Burned to a cedar ash your heart.
Dead, their razzle-dazzle bodies, bare
    Foot in bedroom, pull apart

As things of string. That baited lure
    The flesh, quick and fantastic, thanks
God today; tomorrow, and your
    Tongue tied, dumb mouth of hell. The links

Of love snap. And happiness, once here
    And now, the blood embellished rose,
Declines. They will come home no more,
    Those sailors from the sea, nor those

Soldiers, like yourself, from a far
    Country. You were their wanderlust
Or place of rest. Lack-luster, are
    They as dear as dead? In the past

You waited, excited, watched the door;
    They wait for you forever, not
Caring how long. No new friends wear
    Away your image, nor can plot

You damage. They keep true faith, their
   Loyalty is endless. If a kiss
Woke you sometime, still living, swear
   Love to the dead. A war means this.

II

Death is a soldier and afraid
   Like you. If he could talk, he'd tell
The world how he was hurt. This sad
   Faced, grave eyed, beautiful as steel

Young man, his sex a star, has pride,
   That sharp, unshadowed, surgeon's light
By which heroes are turned inside
   Out, their flamboyant guts put straight

Or lopped off. His dripping wounds bleed
   Acid, salt water, rot the strands
Of cotton gauze and bandages. Blood,
   Blood, blood dapples all our hands

Who lounge through war like girls in bed.
   Camp followers, base bred darlings, hard ·
As our frozen hearts, we loot the dead
   Of their fear, their fearful tears. Word

Of mouth, that snake-pit, says we did
   Our duty. But the lurid gin
Palace, where lust and money collide
   By the bar, then couple in

The gas light, shuts out those who paid
    Not sweetly for our common wealth.
These are no fictions but friends made
    Mock of by heroics. The filth

Which washes them like unction should
    Be for us as well. Soldier, that youth,
A drab death, might have grown great, had
    He been you. To love him, tell the truth.

from *Lament for the Sleepwalker* (1947)

In All the Argosy of Your Bright Hair

Whom I lay down for dead rises up in blood,
Drawn over water after me. His wavering
Footfall echoes from the ocean floor. Blow,
Ye winds, a roundabout. These bully sailors flood
My eyes with tears, treacheries. But his voice shivering
North in lamentation is all I now know—
Whose million miles, once worth gales to be glad,
Tell me last look was best photograph I had.

When that damask duke took my heart for hound,
I dogged him with praises, with poems, a beggar's homage.
His blue eyes, fencing like a dance of swords,
Ringed me from foemen, were night lights. I found
He turned my head from death's entrancing image,
Gold in the desert sun, who sang: "What words
You want, I have." He saved me from my own hand
And the five assassins nervous for the grandstand.

My whole life in gratitude does him no good,
Whose happiness was dancebands, beer, and baseball,
Talked love to be polite. But the soldier boy
Grows up, goes after the goddess in the barbed-wire wood
Who sells him secrets for a firing squad. This tall
Young man, this blond young man, his mother's joy,
Must kill her first, his father next. He shall ride
To the top of the hill where three thieves died.

The whores of Wardour Street, the Soho whores:
"Give us a light, dearie." But I have no match.
Now the inconsolable year hazes with twilight.
Only the cold phantasmal rose burns out-of-doors.
Inside, the lamps are lit. If I should watch

All autumn nights, I'd see no ghost. My light
Fingered friend stole the world away. Imperilled heirs,
You of the equal sadness, give him your prayers.

from *Lament for the Sleepwalker* (1947)

Ovid on the Dacian Coast

Publius Ovidius Naso relegates non exsul
The Decree of Banishment

Airs from the sea blown back,
   The salt wind dense with sedge,
In the surf the sea wrack,
   And rocks ground of the world's edge.

With shells, with bits of quartz,
   With flints, with fragment bones,
Castaway, by dolphin arts,
   He starts, translates the stones.

The marsh birds wheel and shriek
   Above him, as he takes
Word after word from their bleak
   Coast of love: his heart breaks.

In place of gold, he sets
   A banished life between
Driftwood, and out of fish nets
   Roofs his loss with sea green.

Thus lives unexiled, though
   Abandoned, stranded, scanned
By the Dog Star only, for so
   Based, his poems are his own land.

from *Poems: 1950-1974* (1984)

Another of the Same Shepherd's

Waking from worry, he travelled through the morning,
Where doggerel scampered to the formal rocks,
And, circling greener visions, came on flocks
Of ghosts, who, grazing by an arid warning,
Gave him 'Good Sorrow', then returned to scorning
Old memories, while he gathered paradox
In baskets woven from the plaited shocks
Of chance, and chased the black and white suborning.
Noon was still there, waiting by the signpost,
A little bird in his hand, while time of day,
Who had been up since childhood, singing, played.
They walked together, for the rain was lost
Along that road, and praised the lights of May.
And so continued while the waking stayed.

from *Poems: 1950-1974* (1984)

Cardinal Manning

Prince, whom the people praised, though not the great
Men, milling with their money-boxes through
The palaces of chance and keeping state
From slums that opened out their hearts to you—
Your glory blazed through London when you died:
In gold and scarlet, you, etherial, lay
Among the ragged ones, who were your pride,
As you were theirs, even more starved than they.
Your portrait shows you robed in God's own fire
Of love, a skeleton of charity,
Whose eyes, too brilliant for their time, inspire
One most unlike you momentarily
To share the sight you, hungry, could endure:
Christ crucified again in all His poor.

from *Poems: 1950-1974* (1984)

The Artifice of Eternity

The spinning fates
Were kind to Yeats:
They cut his thread
When he was dead:
But not before.

Early he wove
Yellow and mauve
Into a cloth
Which every moth
Easily tore.

He moved his loom
To a public room
Where he could find
The art to wind
His skeins once more.

Then with new skill
He worked until
The pattern showed
How time had flowed
Across the floor.

The weave was tight
Against the light:
The strict design
Of perfect line
Was what he saw.

The thread was spun:
The web was done:
The dyes were fast:
The shroud would last
Which now he wore.

from *Poems: 1950-1974* (1984)

In Rain, in Loneliness, the Late Despair

In rain, in loneliness, the late despair
Of streets like patent leather, where the stop
Light befriends the cigarette-lighting whore,
Her eyes sheltering a whipped mongrel hope;
And buses take their cruel primeval shape,
Mastodons of death grinding through the glare,
Their swimming sockets green with want of sleep;
And the sad city lies cold and wet and poor:
Then I have knowledge, hell is here and now:
How the soul suffers in doorways, is torn
On the iron railings, finds no footing true:
And I am one come from the films to know
No happy end, but that the heart is worn
Out among whores and storefronts and the lack of you.

from *Poems: 1950-1974* (1984)

Passage

The thistles, rooted out, throng in again;
The single regal rose is mobbed by weeds;
The plums, the pears, the ripening apples, rain
In the sun; and past summer plants new seeds.

The chaffinch looks around the world, and takes
His time with August: even wasps relax—
Late afternoon, their metric buzzing breaks
Off, as though they were bees and the light wax.

Here, or there, these common yearly things
Repeat, repeat, and gardens do not range:
Yet thistles, roses, fruit trees, birds, and stings
Come to an end, and the church bells sound a change.

These many soft declensions of the day,
So hard to take to heart, bear life away.

from *Poems: 1950-1974* (1984)

Poem

Eros, his plumes bedraggled by the snow,
Came on me walking through the frozen park.
'Well met,' he said, 'the day is dying now,
So we shall talk together in the dark.'

But there was light enough to see his face,
Those eyes of ice, that mouth impassioned stone,
The whole expressionless, as though a place
Where happiness and suffering were not known.

from *Poems: 1950-1974* (1984)

Magdalen

I

In the delightful cadence of her voice
The wickedness appeared a fragile thing;
But when she spoke, her eyes, like desert fire,
Threw off the darkness of an old waste place;
And if she raised a hand to touch her hair,
The gesture, once it was remembered, stung.
Her odd distracting beauty bore the weight
Of years of jewels and youth grown desolate.

Had any of her flashing friends remained
To question her, the answer, framed in smiles,
Could only have provoked a sullen tear:
Her childhood too had memories to be shunned:
Banal, the usual causeways to despair
Had led her on: she too was one who fails,
Another of the hated self-same kind
Who also weep and have an unquiet mind.

The world she knew was all the world could be—
Charming, deceitful, glazed with colour, cold;
A treasure house disgorging broken beads.
Sometimes her looking-glass threw back a ray
Of night light, and she saw the seven heads
Behind her, each an angel from the wild
Lost land of ruin—evil, avid, smart;
Clever at doing over a child's heart.

In scented shops her taste for trifles soared:
'But have you nothing pleasanter than pearl?'
An air of riches made her misery
Seem for a moment not to have occurred.

For this was never happiness, the slow
Effacement of God's image in her soul.
She aged in spirit: wrinkled there, her grief
At being who she was dreaded relief.

                           II
Music and laughter and the subtle
Deceptive wine:
'Mary, they tell me, is buying a rattle
Instead of an emerald mine.'
And the air on the lyre is collusive,
Love being lost:
'So *that's* why she's turned so evasive.
Dear Mary, a leper at last!'

                          III
Behind the lattic
From the terrace giving on the street,
She waited,
Her terrible face unveiled,
To see the Son of God go by.

He passed in white.
He looked at her.
And in that instant she was cured.

The curtains in the doorways
Tore from their brackets,
As the seven devils left.

The sobs that shook her free from them,
The tears that washed the belladonna off,
The blaze of rings that fell like stars
    Down to the ground—

All these He had forseen forever,
Who now continued on His way
To dinner with the Pharisees.

IV

The perfume had been given her by Herod,
That connoisseur of every lustrous thing;
To him, so bored, so restless, always wearied,
The incongruity at once appealed:
The coronation oil of roses sealed
In alabaster for the Jews' true king,
Let it be squandered on the lovely harlot,
Who burned through life, like a Roman bride, in scarlet

Held in her hands now, the delicate translucent
Jar glowed. Torchlight cascading off the gold
Diadem top rebounded from complacent
Eyes. How the respectable stared at her!
Those properly dressed impeccable diners were
Encouraged in their wooden hearts. This bold
Bad beauty, flaunting a wanton's unbound torrent
Of flaming hair, would find herself abhorrent.

Their heads turned, like the Greeks at games, a society
Of victors. How delightful virtue seemed!
The Man who scourged the bankers from their piety
Knew how to deal with what was so much worse.
Those tears, how easily they ran! His curse
Would dry them soon enough. Ah, but they streamed
Now over His feet! And what did she use for a towel
But hennaed hair. The goggling good had to scowl.

This was too much. His silence should have ended
Sooner. They might be truly scandalized
And never recover. As they contended,

With intense wide-eyed glances, shrivelling smiles,
And shoulders shrugged, to disparage her wiles,
Each hoping to appear the more surprised,
Since the Guest whose feet were stained red mattered
In pious circles, their fierce quiet was shattered.

And the whole room filled with the scent of roses,
As the diadem tinkled to the floor.
So their anointed sovereign, knowing the vices
Which lay among their good deeds, leaned down to
This hopeless unspeakable woman, who,
Acting always in bad taste, bowed to adore
Him, whom they treated with their faint civility,
And praised her now victorious humility.

Simon, their sensitive, their scrupulous leader,
Who felt as though touched by ice when this wild
Debauchee wept, tried to keep back the shudder
Of goodness grazed by her bright brilliant eyes,
As she heard the words only the sinful prize:
'Your sins are forgiven. Go in peace.' And a child,
At whose new-found beauty the angels repeated
Their songs of praise, withdrew from the defeated.

V

High in the noonday sky,
    His arms thrown open wide,
Love is about to die,
    With a thief on either side.

One He has welcomed home,
    The other prefers to hate,
Like the Pharisees, who roam
    In packs and wait and wait.

The soldiers there below,
   Bored and ashamed and blind,
Rattle the dice and throw
   Their lives away like rind.

The mocking scholars toss
   Their beautiful white heads
Far off; but at the Cross
   Who reads?

His mother, calm in pain,
   Adoring, and John,
The youngest friend, remain:
   Fair weather friendships gone.

And one other. She,
   Whose sins have had their share
In blossoming that tree,
   Offers her sorrow there.

Those tears are now for Him,
   Not for herself; she weeps
Outside her life; eyes swim
   Up from their own deeps.

His gift of sacrifice
   Opens her rusted heart:
With Him she pays the price
   Of love, that suffering art.

And so triumphant grief
   Makes her the fourth to stay:
Two innocents, a thief
   And a whore, together pray.

VI

The sun that shone beyond the morning star,
Dispersing night and coldness in the air,
Brought out the hidden birds, brought out the clear
Colour of the rose, brought out the more
Than aromatic fragrance of the myrrh
She carried through the dawn, and lit each tear
That mingled with the dew as she came near
The tomb in which the waiting angels were.
They spoke: she answered, weeping, unaware
Of what their brightness meant, of whom the door
Already must have opened on, so dear
Was He whose absence caused her absent stare.
But then the Gardener gently questioned her:
'Mary!' He said, and she forgot to fear.

VII

At Baume the years had passed in stillness
And many prayers been said.

The dying woman who had lived alone,
Poor,
And blessedly obscure;
Unafraid
Of robbers or the kind of illness
For which nothing can be done;
Now waited while the high horizon lifted;
And in the rift of clouds,
With mist between,
The mountain vistas shifted:
A different scene
Spread out below her.

Above the lonely frightened crowds
Of pagans in the south of France,

Who fled
From every thought of being dead,
And had they had the chance,
Would not have wished to know her;
High in the bright mercurial air,
Poised on her point of vantage,
She gazed
Out on the gorgeous future
Which all the politicians praised,
And watched
The martyrs rising into Heaven
Who bore the marks of torture
Those she had strengthened by a prayer
Said centuries before.

Further, she saw them matched
By other brother saints—
The odd percentage
Who in their simple goodness had forgiven
The costumed fools who cuffed them,
So buffed them
That they shone,
Each, as it were, a moon
In which to see something of Christ's radiance.

Those
In that vast obedience
Whose own
Holiness had grown
In the light that dazzles down
On the Fisherman's heaving blood-red throne,
The haloed Popes
Smiled and blessed
This dying woman of the world.

So she was shown
Through the serpent-circled years:
The tapestries of mail slid back on metal ropes,
And the little wars ran screaming to the serpent's breast
And drank their hatred from its primal source,
Oblivious to a world in tears.
The smoke of burning churches curled
Like money signs
Over the counting houses,
And the dead lay down like dogs
Beneath the bankers' ormolu tables—
Heraldic beasts embossed on cheque-book fables.

Looming beyond the yellow fogs
Spread by the coroneted liars,
The bartered negroes shuffled from the diamond mines:
(Earlier, before the Boston and Bristol slave-buyers):
And other noble causes
Of the golden times in which the present peoples live,
As mothers dragging trucks of coal on hands and knees,
And children skinned alive inside the chimneys of the rich:
Things hard for anyone but God to forgive,
The former friend of Herod saw.

Closer to now
The belching furnace of the buccaneers
Deposited its oily smitch
Over the bankrupt nations, while
The rouge beast nosed aside the broken stile,
In whose retractable-clawed and the file-fanged empires teemed
The terror-struck inheritors of the millionaires—
Those men of mazelike markets, who,
Hidden behind
An iron Venetian blind,
While trafficking with a self-raised demon,

Would pitch their hard bright desks in Hell
Sooner than later,
If there were money to be made there,
And power to be schemed
For, and a soul to sell.

Then,
As she further sickened at the dense
And acrid smell
Of sin,
She prayed
For ice-clad nymph and brassy-hearted satyr,
Who clashed each long-linked fetter
As though its music maddened them,
The old companions of her lonely youth,
That each might see the truth
And far surpass her in their penitence –
Those once rebellious children, now
Indentured to a bitter lust,
Through whose bleak souls the devils danced,
Engrossed in nakedness and desolate desires,
To whom the things of God could make no sense
Until the chains began to rust
That weighted them down in grief-damped fires
Lit in the tinder years of pride.
And the shameless were ashamed.

For as her love for Christ had grown the greater,
Her heart, expanding, rose the lighter
In the rarifying air.
She came to look on others
With His eyes,
And prize
The most disparate people.
He, who had died

To save the crossing-sweeper of Benares
Together with His multitudinous brothers
From Mozambique and Buenos Aires,
The athlete and the cripple,
Willed that the wildest beast of man be tamed—
Nero,
And the latest spiritual zero,
Stalin and Hitler,
And President Attila
Of the Anonymous Bank of Distrust,
And the tiny tyrants too,
At home and office,
In factory and school.
Even the furtive salacious stock-broker
Must not shock her;
Nor the prized pornographic writer
Excite her
To lump him with the calculating cruel,
As belonging to the few
She could not bring herself to love.

All must be seen as having cost
The last drop of Blood
That left God's broken Heart,
Who was not crucified to
Save only the well-thought-of
In the front pew,
But also all who would be lost
If their salvation depended
On the distaste of those who
Had barely chosen the better part.
No one so vile
But God Himself would welcome with a smile
And heap Heaven on,
If he would on his side

Ask to be forgiven,
And be resolved
That this sorrow,
Today and not tomorrow,
Ended
A life spent picking over garbage

In the slums of sin.
Who was she, then,
To falter at loving
Those living
As she had lived herself—
Who might at any moment react to Love
Truly
As she, she thought, had never done?
Had not her sins been there to prove
Daily
The feeding grounds
For wickedness in others?
Had they been given
Through Christ's wounds
Her view of Heaven
Would they be half so faint
At becoming a saint?
Those she had turned away from once
With the sharp disdain of terror,
As she thought of having herself been involved
In their catastrophic error,
She prayed for now
Always with feeling,
And never would allow
Herself to be too tired to plead
For anyone
Whom she had known
At Herod's court,

Hopeful she was not failing
Them in their need—
The far-off friends,
Whom now she loved
As not before.

So, while the pleasure-boats sailed in
And out
Of jewel-like harbours up and down the coast,
And the poor sad rich in speeding cars
Went, heedless, by
The bitter and the destitute,
The red-haired woman at the world's ends,
Kneeling below the stairs,
Prepared to die.

VIII

Back through the ages raced her pulse:
The un-caged heart began to flutter.

Breathless a little
At the sudden subtle
Doubt
Which Lucifer spun out
Of his red-hot
House in Hell
And tried to skitter
Over the light-reflecting sea
Of her soul,
She made it ricochet
In abasement of his pride
By asking the angels at her side
To give her comfort in the combat
Of humility;
'I do not deserve,' she said,

'To pit my mind
Against this blind
Seraph;
Nor will I argue now,
But beg the Lord
To show me how
To thank Him, whom I have seen,
For giving me this grace
To testify
My faith, as though I had not been
Called by His own voice
To consecrate my everlasting choice
Of Him
The day He rose, immortal, from the dead.'

The angels lifted her, encompassed in their light,
And took her to the chapel of Saint Maximin,
Where he received her,
Vested, on his way to Mass.

So Calvary recurred:
And Christ in form of bread and wine
Offered His Body and His Blood for all the world
And for this woman who had loved Him
Splendidly.

Once more she heard
The Centurion's self-forgetful words,
First spoken in the dust of Palestine:
'Lord,
I am not worthy.'
And Christ gave
The white
Sunlight
Circle of Himself—

Proof of His never-ending Love—
To nourish her
Before the great journey.
'Jesus,' she whispered, 'I have found
With my last breath
The way to sound
Your name,
And at my death
How to start
To adore your Heart.'

'Mary!' He said.

So as a bride
To the wedding feast,
Her soul set out
In peace.

IX

All the planets in their seasons sang:
All the stars revolved through arcs of light:
All the galaxies flared up like torches set to guide her home.

Incomparably bright,
She soared along
The avenues of angels
In her Father's Kingdom—

    Angels, Archangels
    Thrones, Dominations,
    Powers, Principalities, Virtues,
    Cherubim
            and
    Seraphim—

Choir upon choir,
Afire
With love,
Those myriad million presences who stand
And carry out the laws
By which the microcosms move,
Obedient in the ecstasy of thought's unbodied nature
To their First Cause
And Unmoved Mover of their wills,
Each beatific creature
Wholly subservient to Him
Whose overflowing goodness fills
Their minds with truth,
To whom their poised magnificence reflects
Facets of that pure peace in which He acts.
These,
And those
From the world's youth:
Her father, Adam,
The forgiven son,
And Eve, her mother,
And all the holy other
Ancestral people—
Abraham,
Who numbered her among his starlike children;
David,
The evil poet who became
A contrite one,
Whose poems, embodied by
The Spirit who can never lie,
Had been the vivid
Means by which her will had grown more supple,
Down on that dot-diminished height
Of pale Provence,

In choosing to be chosen by
The shepherd king's
Divine Inheritor;
Prophets,
To whom the happy future brings
Their ever-present joy,
As they experience all of its
Continuum at once;
Patriarchs,
Young fathers of the now triumphant poor,
Who radiate
From them in meritorious
Points of light;
Unnumbered holy ones from every land
And time,
Of every colour—

The darling boy
Snatched from his mother's arms
And God-forseen terrible harms
By that unmerited convulsive pain
Which won the flying coward
An extravagance of valour,
Never even having to think of sacredness again;
And the old man
Who had served his grasping employers
Without blame,
Prompt to answer the bell,
Been a miser only
Of unkind words,
And with his pennysworth of goodness to the lonely
Bought several statesmen back from Hell;
Having both foregone
In going Heavenwards
The age they left behind,

The thought-resistant child
And the calm survivor with the thought-filled mind,
Now think together,
Each the youthful happy brother
Of one another:

And likewise all the lately
Domiciled
In greatly
Separated centuries—
Those from the smoke-charred caves
And the imperial porcelain graves,
From Nizhni Novgorod,
From either Thebes,
Palmyra, Cuzco, and Peking,
Athens and Atlantic City,
The pigmy palaces among the trees,
The glass-lined laboratories,
And the mud huts raised in bee-hive stories,
Christmas and Easter Islands—

Countless,
They sing
Among
The angles,
Making up the number
Of the rebels,
Those who thought that they were wrecking
Heaven
In their failure
To remember
God's pity
For poor man,
So much lesser
In nature

Than each deep damned angelic creature
Who fell
After his relentless
Un-nimbussed
Leader
Like a counterfeit of lead
On the hard fact
Of Hell.

Now magnified
Through God's humility in having died
For them,
Graced
With glory,
Placed
Like consecration candles
On the walls of Christ's own home
To burn forever
With love,
Their brightness kindles
The cataract
Of light
That pours about them as they praise
God
In the never-ending happy days
That last,
The dream of childhood
They have wakened to,
Immortal kings
Whose crowns were cast
In the fire of suffering here on earth.

Circle on circle
Of these loved kinsmen passed,
As she rose

Towards the height
Of all their songs.

Saint Michael,
Coruscating like the sunlit sea,
Seneschal,
Who welcomes each arriving soul,
Took her to
        Saint Joseph,
Who, standing, in the radiance of his youth,
Beside
        The Queen of heaven,
                Smiled
With the regal innocence of a child,
And looked at her with love.

She,
Whom the world will ever praise,
Virgin and Mother,
Who listens for the slightest casual prayer,
The faintest hopeful mention of her name,
And answers with the best
Thing needed by the sinner in his lair,
The grace to leave it for the open air
Of God's forgiving Heart,
She,
Mere Jewish village girl,
Now
Exalted by her Son above
The loftiest creations of His love,
She,
Whose purity no sin had dared come near,
Threw out her hands in greeting
To the sometime mistress of so many men
The sometime courtesan from Magdala,

Whom Christ,
Her Son
Had drawn
To comfort her
Beside the Cross,
When
In the dark afternoon
He gave
His life that men might live.

To Christ,
The King, the Conqueror,
Seen in the splendor of His risen glory,
   On the right hand of His father,
   And One
   With Him
   And with the Holy Ghost,
She knelt.

'Mary!' He said.
And she was home.

At Baume
Her body waits its joyful resurrection.

Sancta Maria Magdalena,
                ora pro nobis.

Saint Mary Magdalen,
             pray for us.

from *Poems: 1950-1974* (1984)

An Interview with Philip Trower

*Philip Trower was Dunstan Thompson's closest friend and companion. The author of numerous works on the history and doctrine of the Catholic church, as well as two novels (*A Danger to the State *and* Tillotson*), Trower lives in Hertfordshire, twenty miles north of London. This interview was conducted by D. A. Powell and Kevin Prufer via email in 2008-2009.*

————

When did you and Dunstan Thompson meet, and how did your affinity for one another develop?

I was introduced to Dunstan by a friend, Robin Chancellor, whom I had been at school with, some time in February or early March 1945. Robin was the son of a retired governor-general, and we met at a gathering in Mount Street near Grosvenor Square at the flat of a friend of Robin's called Peter Price. Peter was that peculiarly English phenomenon, the son of a rich landowning Labour member of Parliament! Neither Peter nor Robin were in the forces for health reasons. I give these details to convey the ethos and the époque. Dunstan was a GI in the American army, working in the American Office of War Information which was also in Mount Street. Before that he had been working as a GI in a medical unit in East Anglia. (His Harvard friend Harry Brown, at the time a sergeant working for the *Stars & Stripes*, got him the job.) I was a lieutenant in the British army working in London and about to be sent to an intelligence unit in Cairo, Egypt, to complete my war service. After being wounded in the Italian campaign and invalided home, I had been posted to an organisation in London called the Political

Intelligence Department, but was due to be sent to Egypt in a month or two.

But why does one ever become friends with one person rather than another once there are enough interests in common to create an initial affinity? A factor certainly was that I was already trying my hand at writing poetry, as so many young people do without carrying it on beyond their twenties. An influence on me had been the English poet Laurence Whistler, who at one time had been my company commander. But from Dunstan's point of view my efforts must have seemed very jejune and old-fashioned.

This aroused the hidden teacher that was always there in him. He was soon in his always immensely generous way showering me with books by the most recent poets and writers and explaining why I should admire them. We had also both had an education heavily oriented towards the classics and shared a love of history. For neither of us were sports a major interest. We differed chiefly in that his upbringing had been entirely urban while mine had been largely in the country. One could almost say that he only discovered nature in its non-human dimensions after he settled in the English countryside in 1948. The early poems are entirely about human relationships and if some aspect of nature in the wider sense is called on it is analogously not for its own sake.

Reading the early criticism and prose by Dunstan Thompson, one senses a lively, very witty and intelligent young man, one quick to a joke or a judgment—a brilliant, though perhaps sometimes immature, companion. The poems, of course, suggest an altogether different kind of person. Can you tell us about Dunstan Thompson's personality as you knew him?

This is not an easy question to answer. He was such an unusual combination of qualities, characteristics and gifts, some of them at war with each other. If I say that during our many conversations together I sometimes had the impression I was listening to Burke or Dr. Johnson, at others to Sydney Smith or Horace Walpole, and yet others to Newman or Manning, Keats or Coleridge, I am not trying to suggest he was some kind of world genius or necessarily on the same level with any of these famous names; it is only to convey how multifaceted his personality was.

Physically he was for from robust as well as being hyper-sensitive, highly strung and impractical. Some of this seems to have been due to a difficult birth that had left him with a slight tremor in his right hand which came on when he felt nervous

But all that is more physiological than personal. In his poem "Dedication," where he lists what he saw as most characteristic of himself, after "the shyness from my youth" he puts "the gaiety bestowed at birth." (He was using the word in its traditional sense, meaning carefree and merry, loving happiness, laughter, friends and fun, and being easily entranced by what is good in life.) Although he was always deeply aware of the sombre, tragic and fleeting dimensions of human existence—what the ancients summarized as *sunt lacrimae rerum* and *eheu fugaces*, and which permeate much of his poetry—the fun-loving dimension was always there, ready to come to the surface when the time was ripe. I should also add that any shyness rapidly vanished with people he knew well.

His discovery that nothing in this world fully comes up to scratch developed unusually early. At the age of ten or eleven, when his parents took him to see Versailles, not just the palace, but the whole works, his final verdict was "Is that all?"

I suppose I should next come to his intelligence. He was exceptionally clever, but his intelligence was not primarily of the mathematical, logical or syllogistic kind, though he could quickly see the flaw in an argument, and expound ideas with exceptional force and lucidity. It was more imaginative and intuitive. He seemed to know by instinct just why and how human beings behave the way they do in particular situations. It didn't matter whether he was talking about historical figures, men and women in public life or people he knew personally.

At the same time he was highly observant and intensely curious about almost every aspect of what was going on around him. His appetite for newspapers and newsprint of all kinds, ranging from serious periodicals to society magazines, was almost an addiction. It was as though he couldn't know enough about the mysteries, follies, beauties, terrors and dramas of human existence, which throughout his life both fascinated and amazed him.

After intelligence and imagination, I think, must come love of truth and moral courage. In the poem just mentioned he speaks of "devotion to truth" being "my only value as God gives me worth." It wasn't so much a matter of not telling lies. We all like to think we are truthful in that sense. It meant wanting to get to the heart of things and facing up to them just as they are. This is where his Dr. Johnson side came in. If he thought something seriously false or wrong had been said, he could be formidable. It didn't matter whom he was talking to. After his death three of four people, who were genuinely fond of him, told me that at these times they could be quite frightened. But these formidable outbursts never lasted long, and he was always one of the first to laugh at himself when he had been silly or apologise if he had been unjust.

Perhaps "mercurial" is the best word for describing the surface of his personality, but it was a surface overlying, in intellectual things, a powerful will and a bedrock of strong convictions and attachment to what one of his Harvard teachers called the "eternal verities."

Putting it another way one could say that he managed to be both a realist and a romantic simultaneously. This only presents a problem I think for people who see the two terms as necessarily a dichotomy. In using the word romantic about Dunstan, I simply mean that his realism included being responsive at the same time to the "magic" and mystery of life, which is also part of the "way things are." It is a matter of two dimensions of one and the same reality, not two contradictory approaches.

What did he do during the war? How did the war affect him?

He could hardly have been more ill-adapted physically and psychologically to any kind of military life. Through the influence of his father, a senior naval officer, he started by trying his luck at an officer training camp, but failed to pass. He was then successively (first as a GI and then as a corporal) for 8 months or so in the US followed by just over two years in England and a final 6 months in Paris. Most of the time he seems to have been attached to base camps or working in offices. He never saw combat of any kind, though he was in London at the height of the bombing. Of his fellow GIs he always said they never showed him anything but kindness. It was probably because he was so very different and impractical. His continual need of help seemed always to bring out the best instincts in them. Had he been more ordinary he might have had a rougher time. Of some of the officers he was less appreciative. All these experiences must have influenced his outlook on life to some degree. But I cannot say they left any noticeable marks or scars.

What did affect him was the year and a half he spent in London, and, as Eliot wrote in a letter to Conrad Aiken, getting to know "all the right people there in two seconds flat." The right people meant mainly the top literati of the time, people like the Sitwells, the Spenders, Cyril Connolly and so on.

Since he never saw combat, how might he have described the source of the world-weary, combat fatigued voice that one finds in so many of his early poems?

You have to remember that being in London during the bombing had aspects of being in the front line. However there was another side to him. He could treat the bombing very debonairly. I also remember him telling me how at the time he had this illusory sense of quasi immortality. The bombs might hit other people but not him.

Who were his models, literary or otherwise?

I don't think I could say he ever took anyone as a model. He was in his own way too independent-minded. It was more a question of influences. Obviously of special importance were his teachers at Harvard, particularly Robert Hillyer and Ted Spenser, both poets themselves. For Hillyer he had a special affection. After that, at least in chronological order, comes Conrad Aiken. In the summers of 1938 and 1939 he spent a month with Conrad Aiken and his wife at Rye in England. They ran a summer school there in creative writing. In Aiken's *Collected Letters* there are some references to Dunstan, indicating Aiken's early recognition not so much at this point of his poetic talent as of his cleverness and intelligence. Aiken introduced him to Eliot whom he visited in London in both years. For Eliot he always had great respect and admiration, even if it was tinged at times with the kind of humourous affection one often feels when young for older relations. This is best seen in the long poem "Images and Reflections" which appeared in the *Paris Review* in the late 50s, one of the last of his poems to be published during his lifetime. The only other significant influence I can think of was George Barker. They met in New York some time between 1939 and 1942 when Dunstan was drafted into the army. They saw a lot of each other and Dunstan admired him greatly at this time.

Did he talk much about his writing to you? Can you say something about his feelings about his own work, his process as a writer?

I'm afraid the answer is very little. I can remember only one or two casual remarks, often jocular, like saying he had at least one thing in common with Yeats, that he counted the number of stresses in a line on his fingers. He also used to quote Yeats' dictum "Work without toil is the great temptation of the artist." On another occasion I remember him saying rather sadly that poetry was the most difficult of the arts in that while in painting and music you often had works which were at the same high level or even perfect throughout, with poetry this was hardly ever so. He gave as an example of complete success of this kind William Johnson Cory's translation "They told me Heraclitus..." from the Greek Anthology. I do remember that with many of his poems a first draft would lie in a drawer of his desk for a long time being worked over at intervals before he was satisfied with it.

Although Dunstan Thompson wrote fine poems throughout his lifetime, he mostly stopped publishing them after Lament for the Sleepwalker. *What happened?*

He didn't stop publishing. He couldn't get them published. Throughout the 1950s and 1960s he kept sending one new collection of poems after another to his New York agent Margot Johnson without success in spite of her efforts and those of friends like Billy Abrahams, who I think was working at that time for Viking Press. These separate collections are bound together as one in what I call *The Red*

Book (Poems 1950-1974). I had them privately printed just as he arranged them. A half dozen or so of these poems appeared in periodicals like the *New Yorker*, the *Paris Review* and Marguerite Caetani's *Botteghe Oscure*, but that was all. How to account for this, I don't know. A change in public taste? But of what kind? Certainly a change in his own style began around 1948. It became more variegated and less "baroque," so to speak. The subject matter also became greatly extended in range. But that in itself does- n't seem a sufficient explanation.

I'd like to know more about Thompson's literary friendships. Did he keep in touch with Eliot, the Sitwells, Spender, etc., or did he grow reclusive? It seems that the latter is what is implied. And yet, he sought publication…. Surely, he had some idea of a readership inside of ·the literary world?

After Dunstan moved to the country in 1948, he contin- ued to visit London for the day from time to time in order to have lunch with friends, literary and otherwise, though not all that often. In the 1950s it was about a four hour journey each way to London. However, I cannot think of a single friend who, right up to his death, he ceased to see or correspond with, and occasionally they came to stay for a weekend. I remember visits from, among others, Howard Nemerov, Alan Pryce Jones (editor of the *Times Literary Supplement*) and Paul Dehn, an English poet and journalist of the time. (The only exception is George Barker. Dunstan and George had been exceptionally close in London and New York during the war, but later drifted apart.) The word "reclusive" gives the wrong impression. What one can I think say is that after he moved to the country and later recovered his faith, he lost his taste for literary London as he had known it. It is difficult, of course, completely to ignore the literary world if you want to succeed as a poet, nor did he. But I think he would have said he was aiming beyond or outside it, which may have been the cause of the difficulties.

Can you describe Dunstan Thompson's life after, say, 1950? Where did he go? What were his interests? Did he have work outside his writing?

After 1948 when he settled in England in a village on the east coast called Cley-next-the-sea, in the county of Norfolk, he rarely went away, except for occasional visits to London and elsewhere to stay with friends, or day trips to Norwich or Cambridge to buy books. An exception was the trip he made to Rome in 1950 for the Holy Year, followed by visits to Assisi, Ravenna and Venice. This was the last time he left England. But he was not a recluse. Throughout the 1950s and 1960s American friends would come and stay when visiting Europe. Nor did he ever make any fixed plan or decision not to return to the States. It was just the way things turned out. There were two possibly contributing factors. At that time living in the States was much more expensive than in England and on top of it he lost quite a bit of money in the late fifties through the mishandling by a lawyer of some properties he owned. There was also the question of where he was to live. I think he had a feeling that a return to New York might lead him back into his old disorganised way of life.

After his time in the army, he never did anything other than write. In addition to his poems he wrote three more novels and a play about the Elizabethan Catholic martyr Blessed Edmund Campion. None of these found a publisher. Only one of the novels and the play survive.

Apart from reading, which was almost an occupation, recreations were mostly simple and undramatic. The pattern of each day generally included a walk towards the sea or inland up the valley. Later, when his health began to go downhill I would take him for a drive in the car. He loved window shopping in Holt and Sheringham, the nearest small towns to Cley. The antique shops were a special attraction. Sheringham and Cromer, the next town along the coast, which had been fashionable seaside resorts before WW I, provided the inspiration for the long poem "Edwardian Seascape with Figure," which is full of his sense of history, and of subtle amused satire on the resort's rise and decline. He knew a small circle of educated local people and for a time played bridge. But his favourite hobby was modelling in Plasticine, copying figures from books about classical and renaissance sculpture.

Then of course there was conversation. Before supper each day we had a "happy hour" when we discussed what we had been reading or thinking about, or what was going on in the world, locally and internationally. In the last two years of his life I took rough notes of some of the things he said which I hope to transcribe when I have finished the full length memoir.

The critic Dana Gioia has suggested that Dunstan Thompson was one of the great mid-century American Catholic poets. How did Dunstan Thompson's relationship to his faith evolve over the years?

To begin at the beginning, he had the most intensely Catholic upbringing of anyone I have ever met. He used to say of his parents that they would both have died for the faith but would have mounted the scaffold from opposite sides!

By this he meant that his father, who had been educated in France, had a rather austere Cistercian-like approach to his religion while his Mother's piety might be called "Italian baroque." His mother's influence, at least in early life, was the stronger.

Because of the social position of his mother's family in the Washington Catholic world, from his earliest years he was used to meeting members of the higher clergy, cardinals included, serving their masses and listening to higher ecclesiastical chitchat. But more important was the instruction he received at his Catholic schools. In those days the faith was taught without any "ifs" and "buts" and with a strong Thomistic or scholastic matrix and substructure. Although the latter has come in for a lot of criticism since the 2nd Vatican Council in the 1960s, it left its hearers with a clear grasp of what the Church expected them to believe, as well as providing them with the rudiments of a solid philosophical formation.

All this continued until at the age of seventeen, under the usual pressures exerted by puberty, he started to become less devout and eventually gave up the practice of his religion. I use this expression rather than saying "lost his faith" because, at least to begin with, it was a matter of morals, not intellectual uncertainties. Of course any Christian who gives up praying and keeping one or other of the Commandments is soon going to be plagued by more and more doubts. But there is a difference between people who give up their Christianity because of intellectual difficulties and those for whom moral problems come first. Dunstan belonged to the latter class. For such there is nearly always in the back of their minds the thought that were life to get too bad there is always the Church as a last resort. Even when he was seemingly furthest from the Church, he often told me, he never allowed anyone to run it down in his presence.

I say all this because I believe that if the early poems should ever be subjected to a sufficiently close analysis, it will be seen that only a lapsed Catholic of the second kind could have written them. I feel as sure as anyone can be about things of this sort that both some of the imagery and a proportion of the attitudes and responses will bear this out. I would say the preoccupation with death—much more than in other war poets—and the way it is handled is an example.

He remained away from the Church or unpracticing for the next fourteen years, that is until 1952 when the return took place. However, looking back, I can see many signs or symptoms of a return before that.

When the changes began after the 2nd Vatican Council in 1952 he accepted the new liturgy because it came from the Successor of St. Peter, without believing popes to be infallible in anything except faith and morals. But he strongly opposed the maverick theologians who were pressuring the Church to change fundamental doctrines. Indeed at the time of his death he was working on a book designed to explain the roots of the crisis.

What else was he working on at the end of his life? Whose work was he reading? Did he have literary models he held to throughout his life?

After 1967, as I mentioned, his health began to decline, so he couldn't do as much as before. But he was still writing or revising poems up until about a fortnight before he died. The kinds of books he read didn't change much from the mid-fifties on. Apart from religious books it was still mainly history and biography, with a smattering of psychology and for light relief the usual supply of newspapers and magazines.

The only figure I can think of who could in any sense be described as a model was Keats. How much Keats influenced his poems is for better qualified people to decide. But he loved Keats as a person. He frequently re-read his letters, except for the last half dozen or so which he kept unread so that he would always have them to look forward to. Strangely enough there is a portrait of Keats sitting reading in a chair which is strikingly like him to look at. I am not implying any parity of gift. It is just an odd co-incidence seeing how devoted he was to him.

What Became of Dunstan Thompson?
by Edward Field

Gay scholar and poet David Bergman called him the gayest poet of World War II, and National Endowment for the Arts chief Dana Gioia called him the best Catholic poet of the latter half of the 20th Century. This is Dunstan Thompson, who has always been one of my favorite poets. But, today, who has ever heard of him?

When I discovered Dunstan Thompson's poetry, it was actually not very long after I had discovered poetry when I was a young soldier. And I met him only once, unforgettably, shortly after my discharge from the military at the end of World War II. It was a mystery that, after his youthful success with two books of poems published in the U.S. and one in England to extraordinary acclaim, Dunstan Thompson disappeared from the literary world, as dramatically as if a kingfisher flashed electric blue in the sunlight before diving into a pool, never to reappear. I would not learn the story of the rest of his life until many years later.

In 1943, after Basic Training in Miami Beach, I was in a line of soldiers boarding a troop train for a slow journey of several days across the country to an unknown destination, when a Red Cross lady handed each of us a bag of necessities for the trip, containing toothbrush, comb, candy bar—and a paperback book. The book in my bag

---

Among Edward Field's many books are *After the Fall: Poems Old and New* (University of Pittsburgh Press, 2007), *Kabuli Days: Travels in Old Afghanistan* (World Parade Books, 2008), and *The Man Who Would Marry Susan Sontag, and Other Intimate Literary Profiles of the Bohemian Era* (University of Wisconsin Press, 2005).

was, fatefully, a Louis Untermeyer anthology of great poems of the English language, which I devoured during the long hours of being shunted onto sidings. Three days later, when I got off that train, I knew what I wanted to be: a poet—despite the fact that at age eighteen I had never written a line, and had never known anyone who could conceivably have been called a poet. Of course, in my town writing poetry would have labeled you a sissy. But the army had liberated me from all that.

That anthology was essentially the sum total of my knowledge of poetry until two years later when, wearing my new silver wings, I navigated a B-17, one of the famous Flying Fortresses, across the North Atlantic to an airbase in England. (The trick was not to follow the radio beam the Germans had set up in Sweden to lure you to the wrong destination, and captivity.) My best buddy in another plane in the squadron was a sexy, prematurely bald fellow navigator, with whom I was secretly in love. Dave had gone to Cornell and was cynical about everything. When I confessed to him that Rupert Brooke, the blond, beautiful writer of "If I should die, think only this of me: / That there's some corner of a foreign field / That is forever England," was my favorite poet, he laughed scornfully and said that the greatest modern poet was T. S. Eliot. I'd never heard of him. When he showed me "Prufrock" and "The Waste Land," I didn't have a clue what they were about!

My real introduction to modern poetry came on an airbase in the Midlands, two hours north of London, from which I was flying bombing missions over Germany. After an exhausting daylong flight I would go to the Officers' Club on the base and drink whiskey sours to unwind. There at the bar I met my first real poet ever. A gnome-like young lieutenant with a crooked smile and a beak of a nose that he claimed reflected his aristocratic Anglo-Saxon origins, Coman Leavenworth had already published poems in literary magazines. As a ground officer with a less demanding schedule than us fly-boys, he got down to London regularly, where he frequented London's famous writers' drinking club, the Gargoyle. Over drinks in the Officers' Club I would hang on his reports about the poets he met there, not only the English poets George Barker and Stephen Spender, but the Americans, among them Harry Brown and Dunstan Thompson. The Americans, in and out of uniform, were working either for *Stars & Stripes*, the newspaper of the U.S. Army, or for the Office of War Information—appropriately cushy jobs for such talented men from Harvard.

Under Coman's influence I bought their poetry books. I nearly memorized George Barker's *Noctambules*, a now-forgotten poem that began, thrillingly in that era of persecution of homosexuals and near-blackout of gay writing, with the unforgettable words: "The gay paraders of the esplanade, the wanderers in time's shade…" I already knew what he was talking about there, for most of my sexual experiences had been, necessarily, pickups in the dark. I also knew a little book of Dylan Thomas that included the bracing lines, "my wine you drink, my bread you snap." Stephen Spender, whom I would meet several years later— his hand was on my leg in no time—also became an immediate favorite. But it was Dunstan Thompson's poems that really knocked me for a loop, with lines like "The red-haired robber in the ravished bed," "The boy who brought me beauty brought me death," and "Waiting for the telephone to ring / Watching for a letter in the box." And I'm still dazzled by those flagrantly open paeans and elegies to his affairs with doomed sailors, soldiers, and airmen.

In December 1945, a year after my arrival in England, a year during which I helped bomb the hell out of German cities and discovered, along with poetry, the vast homosexual underground in the armed services, on and off the base, I returned to America on an aircraft carrier whose flight deck crumpled under battering North Atlantic gales.

One of the first things I did after getting home was to contact Dunstan Thompson, who was also now back in the States. Still wearing my silver wings and battle ribbons on my Eisenhower jacket—a recent addition to the uniform that hugged the body fetchingly and led Coman to say with his dirty grin that the top brass must have been horrified when they realized they'd allowed such a seductively revealing uniform to replace the modest, pleated dress jacket— and with a white silk scarf around my neck, a dashing note that fliers had adopted in the War, I met Dunstan for drinks at the 1-2-3 Club on New York's Upper East Side, where a cocktail pianist tinkled away in the background to the subdued conversation at the tables. It was a new world for me, this world of sophistication to which Dunstan belonged.

The perfect aesthete, Thompson had a wonderful dome of a head with bulging eyes and a minimal chin, and waved his long delicate fingers expressively—a dead ringer for a drawing of Keats in the National Portrait Gallery in London. I was in awe. He did nothing to disguise the fact that he was gay, justified by his high aesthetic pose. It was only because the poetry world was such a tiny one that he could get away with using the word "gay" with abandon in his poems, though as a word for homosexual it was not yet in general use. More common were expressions "like that" and "queer," as well as the uglier "pansy" and "fairy." Dunstan, with his Harvard education, was at a stage of cultural development I could never hope to reach.

As it turned out, this cocktail hour was to be our only contact. While being propositioned by Dunstan flattered me, I used to reject most such overtures, preferring casual pickups, however more dangerous. My Officers' Club buddy Coman also dropped out of my life, though many years later, when I sent him a notice of my first book of poems, he replied with a condescending note that referred distastefully to the book as a commercial proposition. Protected by his family's money from the "commercial" world of poetry publishing with its rivalries and ambitions, he seems to have kept his purity by retreating behind the protecting walls of his Park Avenue apartment. But I'm sure he went on writing, and hope that one day his poetry will appear in print.

I don't recall how I heard about Dunstan's death in 1975, but some time after that I started mulling over the idea of editing a new edition of his poems. For a start, I wrote a brief appreciation, including a sampler of his poems, for *Poetry Pilot*, the newsletter of the Academy of American Poets, which came to the attention of Philip Trower, Dunstan's surviving partner. I'd never heard about any partner before, so of course I was curious to explore this further. During a stay in London, after my boyfriend Neil and I had settled into a rented flat, I contacted Trower, who was living in a remote village on the North Sea, and invited him down to London. A kindly man who said he worked as a Vatican reporter for Roman Catholic publications, Trower immediately demystified Dunstan's disappearance, and told me it was "simply" that Dunstan had returned to the Catholic Church—though it didn't sound so simple to me.

He did fill in some other gaps, however. In 1948, under contract with the British publisher John Lehmann, Dunstan had flown to the Middle East to write a travel book, later published in England as *The Phoenix in the Desert*, which I still find impressive for the opening sequence describing his early transatlantic flight, as well as its portrait of the luxurious life of the British colonial class in Cairo, soon to be wiped away forever by Nasser's revolution. It was in Egypt that Dunstan connected with Philip

Trower, who was posted there with the British Forces. Apparently repentant after his youthful hell-raising, Dunstan had retired with Trower, who converted to Catholicism himself, to the seaside village of Cley-Next-the-Sea in Norfolk to be near the shrine of Our Lady of Walsingham. Trower had remained there after his partner's death.

I spoke to him of my puzzlement at never seeing any poems of Dunstan's in print after those early books, except for one poem in the *New Yorker* in the 1950s. Trower assured me that Dunstan had never stopped writing poetry, and that he (Trower) was in the process of putting together a collection of this later poetry. When I finally read the fat, posthumous collection, *Poems 1950-1974*, which left out the already published work from 1943 to 1949, it was clear that religion had transformed Dunstan from brilliant bad boy to repentant sinner. The formal structure was still there, but gone was the defiant glitter of the language, the outrageously gay love poems to soldiers and sailors and airmen in World War II. Now there was weeping and breast-beating as he reviewed his life, wallowing in his guilt, along with "devout" poems of adoration.

I'm still not comfortable with talk of "spirituality" and "the spiritual," and these later religious poems were not at all to my taste. Over the years I've seen a lot of poets bucking for sainthood of a kind, most of them going in for one of the religions of the Orient. But there were others like Dunstan who, unaccountably to me, merely stuck to or returned to the religion they were raised in. I don't necessarily dismiss them as more misguided than the others, but tend to view them as brainwashed from birth. From the evidence of his later poems, Dunstan Thompson—who was raised a Roman Catholic—after indulging his youthful hormones, albeit with a healthy dose of guilt showing even then, was more conflicted than ever. I suspect he never really resolved the issue of his sexuality and his religion, or indeed his poetry and his religion.

But these later poems spilled a lot of beans about his life. He actually came from a world that encompassed wealthy relatives in Newport, Rhode Island, and High Church officials in Maryland. He accompanied his devout mother on visits to these Princes of the Church and got quite an indoctrination into the aristocratic side of Catholicism. On the other hand, once he went away to Harvard, he cut loose, and the riotous atmosphere of the War years abroad gave him a thorough introduction to the pleasures of "Satan." At Harvard he got to know the aspiring writers Harry Brown and William Abrahams. Brown, like Dunstan, landed a cushy job in wartime London, where my ground officer friend, Coman Leavenworth, met them at the Gargoyle and, when he came back to our airbase, reported the juicy details to me—how Spender claimed he'd had boys from every state in the union, the stormy scenes in taxis between Harry Brown and his wife Ursula, etc.

Brown later wrote the war novel *A Walk in the Sun*, which was made into a successful film and led to a career as a screenwriter. Abrahams, who spent the war as an MP in Miami, went on to a distinguished career in publishing, with his own imprint, edited the O'Henry Award series for several decades, and wrote historical books with his partner, the Stanford historian Peter Stansky. Dunstan wasn't quite a recluse in his North Sea village, for his old friends continued to visit him there.

Whatever Trower's "simple" version of Dunstan's transformation—not "conversion" to Catholicism, he corrected me, but "return"—I couldn't help but suspect that the only believable explanation for him to have changed so suddenly was that he had to have had a nervous breakdown. Or, I theorized, back in the 50's, before the

Wolfenden Amendment decriminalized consensual gay sex between adults, he may have been arrested, as so many gays in England were—actor John Gielgud and dancer-choreographer John Cranko come to mind—and the humiliation drove him back to the church. But when I dared to suggest this, Trower told me in his reserved manner that was not the case, that it was simply the effect of Dunstan's turning devout gradually over several years.

With the return to the church, Trower assured me, Dunstan had also renounced worldly activities, including his poetry career, and as the new poems accumulated, unpublished, he'd let the memory of his first books, and his growing reputation, fade. In fact, Trower told me, Dunstan made it quite explicit—and this was the bombshell that sunk my idea to rescue his poetry from oblivion—that he did not want his early poems reprinted even after his death, and Trower, his literary executor, was following his instructions by limiting the new volume to poetry from the devout years, 1950-1974. I'm afraid I had already violated Dunstan's wishes when I published the appreciation in *Poetry Pilot*.

It seems quite curious to me that Dunstan Thompson, who sacrificed his ambitions as a poet to strive for holiness, appears in one of his poems to condemn the equally devout T. S. Eliot, an Anglican, for his success in positioning himself as the King of Poetry, while he supported Conrad Aiken, who believed that he should have been the Anointed One. Aiken, who published many well-received books of poetry in his lifetime and is now pretty much dismissed, justly in my view, is mostly memorable as one of several poets whose lives were scarred by the violent death of a relative: Lucille Clifton, who found her mother murdered in her Baltimore project apartment; Thom Gunn, who came home from school to find his mother hanging in the clothes closet; and Aiken, whose mother shot his father, leading to a messy murder trial during his adolescence.

What happened to "the gayest poet of World War II" whose poems almost all had the word "gay" in them? Nothing Trower said adequately explained this transformation. It just may be that the brilliant young poet, the star of my youth, really was struck by a lightning bolt of some kind. Trower, however, made it clear that Dunstan would not have wanted to be included in any anthology of gay poets or labeled such, and I, too, a survivor of that era, am sure that Dunstan would have been opposed to it, as would May Swenson or any of the other gay and lesbian poets of my generation, except perhaps Adrienne Rich. We saw ourselves part of the austere, the greater world, of Modern Poetry. The gay movement, with supremely confident "out" poets, would bristle at this as a denial, but I think the literary establishment still would agree that it's demeaning for a serious poet to be called anything but simply a poet.

And as a Catholic poet? Dunstan Thompson in his later mode, when many of the poems were on religious themes, could perhaps have accepted that label—like Gerard Manley Hopkins, being Catholic and gay are hardly incompatible. It's just that the Church doesn't seem to understand that yet. Nor did Dunstan himself, who suffered over it to the end.

Memories of Dunstan Thompson
A letter from Sanford Gifford

My earliest & longest-lasting memories of Dunstan concern his sarcastic wit, directed at all & sundry, including us, his circle of close friends on the editorial board of the *Harvard Monthly*. And yet when I try to recall an example, I can only come up with his mocking tone & talent for mimicry. When my ex-roommate would join us, Dunstan would say, "Why Charles, we were just singing your praises!" What made this funny, as well as cruel, must have been his delivery, his tone of voice. He also had a novelistic gift for creating dramas out of commonplace events & acquaintances, such as Why does Robert Davis, our composition instructor sit only with a mirror behind him? His fear of the Secret Police, suspicious of his Marxian sympathies.

His sarcasm created some protest when he published his satirical essay "Fragrant Futility" on the Cowley Fathers' monastery on Memorial Drive. He had charmed his way into their confidence, & they felt betrayed when he made fun of their High-Church efforts to be more Catholic than their Episcopal denomination. His own Catholic background made him the perfect critic, & we always felt that Dunstan's Catholicism was derived from an aristocratic tradition related to his father's high-ranking Naval career & his descent from Count Rumford, the Tory scientist of the Colonial Era.

Sanford Gifford was born in 1918 and educated at Harvard University and the Northwestern University Medical School. He served in the Army Medical Corp in the SW Pacific until 1946 and, since then, has lived in the Boston area, where he has worked on the faculty of the Boston Psychoanalytic Institute and Harvard Medical School.

I have no memory of when Dunstan joined the *Monthly*, a revival created by Herschel Berman of a 19th century student publication that had folded during the First World War. It had many distinguished former editors, from E.E. Cummings to John Dos Passos, whom Herschel believed we could exploit for donations. I also have no idea why Dunstan chose the *Monthly*, rather than the more traditional literary magazine, *The Harvard Advocate*. He quickly became its star, however, & wrote prolific poems, book reviews & extended set-pieces during 1937-38, when he became president. A major satirical essay took issue with Mrs. Jack Gardner & her revered private museum, & another foresaw "The Battle for Harvard Yard" in a fantasy of a fascist future. All Harvard poets wrote about the Spanish Civil War in 1937 for the Boylston Prize, & we were all amazed that Dunstan did not win it.

I remember Dunstan's decision to leave Harvard without graduating, & his fierce pride in applying for a passport with "Occupation: Writer," not "student." He soon returned from England, his would-be literary destination, & I have had short encounters with Dunstan in several locales. First, he spent most of the summer of 1939 with me in Madison, Wisconsin, where I was in summer-school, & again on two summers in San Miguel Allende, an art-school in Mexico created by American & Mexican artists. My younger brother was enrolled in the school, where we visited & traveled around Mexico together afterward, accompanied by Katherine Kuh, a Chicago art-critic whose sarcastic wit was a match for Dunstan's. We repeated the experience the following summer, with another Harvard classmate, & drove from San Miguel to New York City in the car of the school's director, Cossio del Pomar, an aristocratic Peruvian revolutionary. Three passengers & the driver meant that one of us took turns in the rumble-seat, where we were drenched in tropical downpours. Dunstan took his turn, but made great fun of his attempts to dodge his obligation.

In many ways Dunstan was the ideal traveling companion, intensely curious & observant about everything we saw, & equipped with the historical background to make dramatic sense of it. This is born out by his later travel writing, like *The Dove with a Bough of Olives*, but traveling with him was an indescribable light-hearted experience, with his high spirits, sense of humor & optimism in encountering obstacles.

My wife Ingrid & I had a last series of visits from Dunstan when we were in medical school in San Francisco & he would come up from Fort Ord. As a draftee in boot-camp, he was not happy with military discipline, but he made fun of his hardships & found a suggestible bunkmate who would shine his shoes in return for poetry-readings. This was a *tour-de-force* no other unhappy literary draftees of my acquaintance could have managed successfully.

Many years later Ingrid & I, with our two young sons, made a summer visit to Dunstan & Philip Trower at Cley-next-the-Sea, East Anglia. On the beach of flint pebbles the size of marbles, with a cold wind blowing off the North Sea, I asked Dunstan what it was like in winter. Not very different, he told us, but he never complained about the British chill, even though his cheeks were acquiring the mottled purple of a true Englishman, which he had indeed become.

This brief account of my contacts with Dunstan omits the most important element of our lifelong friendship, his irrepressible flow of animated conversation, in person & in correspondence. Much of it was about books & poetry, but also about politics, world events & our many mutual friends. He remembered them, naturally, as they once were, & his prodigious memory included details that many of us

had forgotten, as if our early years together were pre-
served in amber.

All the best,
Sanford Gifford

PS: An absurd anecdote about Dunstan comes back to
mind. During his years at Harvard, there was a peculiar
screening process, compulsory silhouettes of posture
decreed by the famous anthropologist (I forget his name)
of the ectomorph-mesomorph-endomorph classification.
Those who flunked it, like me & Dunstan & a few other
literary types, were condemned to special gym classes with
a Mr. Fradd, ageless & rubbery-muscled who tossed
around a medicine-ball, grotesquely heavy, as if it were a
basketball. Dunstan plotted a method of getting out of
this compulsory class: a totally imaginary encounter with
Mr. F, who had floored him with a medicine-ball, humili-
ating him before the class & creating a traumatic neurosis
that should excuse him from class. The dean, however,
outwitted Dunstan by relieving him from class attendance
but assigning him instead to one-to-one sessions with Mr.
F himself. In short this was not a triumph for Dunstan, but
it illustrates his imaginative skills.

Lovelorn at First Read:
On Discovering Dunstan Thompson
by Kolt Beringer

"No one is here. I am my own best friend."
—from *"The Prince, His Madness, He Raves at Mirrors"*

Whenever visiting my home city, Minneapolis, Minnesota, I make a point to stop by Magers & Quinn Booksellers on Hennepin Avenue and peruse their poetry collection, hoping for some rare find. On one such trip, as I walked up and down the aisles, reading the poets' names off the spines of books, it seemed as though the shelves held every known poet—from Anna Akhmatova to James Wright, and from Adrienne Rich to T. S. Eliot—but then I came across an ocean-blue-colored spine that bore the name Thompson and the title *Lament for the Sleepwalker*.

Intrigued, I pulled the book from the shelf and randomly opened it to the Petrarchan sonnet, "This Tall Horseman, My Young Man of Mars," where the speaker laments the interplay of love and deception between him and his lover:

This tall horseman, my young man of Mars,
Scatters the gold dust from his hair, and takes
Me to pieces like a gun. The myth forsakes
Him slowly. Almost mortal, he shows the scars
Where medals of honor, cut-steel stars,
Pin death above the heart. But bends, but breaks

Kolt Beringer is an assistant managing editor at HarperCollins Publishers. He earned his MFA at Columbia University School of the Arts in 2007. He lives in Brooklyn, New York.

In his hand, my love, whose wrecked machinery makes
Time, the inventor, weep through a world of wars.

In the first quatrain, the speaker compares his lover to a
Roman warrior god: when the lover takes his helmet off
and shakes his golden locks, gold dust settles around
him—and the speaker becomes weak, unequal to his lover.
However, as the speaker continues describing his "young
man of Mars," the reader learns that the lover is quite
human after all. So much so, that with each victory, the
lover withdraws and his heart darkens, bearing the weight
of death. In the second quatrain, the mythic comparison
breaks down, as the lover's persona changes from a warrior
to a soldier and love turns to ruin.

In the sonnet's sestet, the speaker further dismantles
his lover's image: a casual, common mortal whose fleeting
need is only to be pleasured—nothing more, nothing less.
The power roles reverse, the speaker becoming stronger
than the warrior. This relationship built on casual encoun-
ters weighs heavily upon the speaker and is ultimately what
drives the two apart, as the speaker desires a long-term,
respectable communion with another:

Guilt like rust enamels me. I breed
A poison not this murdering youth may dare
In one drop of blood to battle. No delight
Is possible. Only at parting do we need
Each other; together, we are not there
At all. Love, I farewell you out of sight.

I leaned against the bookshelf and reread the poem; I was
delighted. Thompson's poetic diction and vivid imagery
ignited the page. That day I felt as though I had unearthed
a master lost, one unabashedly romantic but never apolo-
getic. I read another poem and another—each title and
poem equally as thrilling as the one it preceded: "In All the

Argosy of Your Bright Hair," "A Knight of Ghosts and
Shadows," "Nor Mars His Sword," "The Everlasting
Gunman," and "This Life, This Death."

Love and mutilation—figuratively, metaphorically—
become the reigning themes throughout the collection as
Thompson recounts life's infinite and minute troubles; the
pleasures of love and its often problematic aftermath are
equated with death, whether on the battlefield or in the
hospital, as one might expect, or in the pub or in a garden.
His poems exhibit a verbal texture in both timbre and
imagery, which tease and elicit emotion throughout each
poem, as in:

> Death blows your boys to ribbons. They were
> Your friends. Their eyes like lapis glow
>
> With stone-cold brilliants, eyes whose fire
> Burned to a cedar ash your heart.
> >   —"Songs of the Soldier"

And:

> Now when the fire fails and the loneliness kills
> And the soul longs to be gone from where it is,
> I appear bemused to you, wondering—would a kiss
> Make the gesture, or change of feature? How these miles
> Between us freeze, sparkling through darkness.
> >   —"A Knight of Ghosts and Shadows"

Further:

> But now the stars of heaven sail like ships
> Above the trees, and round about your house .
> Ancestral ghosts are wandering, long come home
> From war and voyages. Now this garden sleeps . . .
> >   —"The Moment of the Rose"

Individual poems—and the entire collection—as much as

they embrace the deaths of fellow comrades and relation-ships, are structured to carry out a singular mission: bring order to chaos caused by love and war. The reader comes to find a true companion in an honorable master. And so after all has been remembered and revealed, Thompson imparts one final consolation: "We dream / Of the rose and happiness, we dream until / The end of love is that the heart is still" ("The Moment of the Rose").

I was lovelorn at first read.

On July 5, 2005, I purchased Thompson's out-of-print first edition, *Lament for the Sleepwalker*, for $12.83. (I still have the receipt leafed in the edition like a bookmark. Later, I would purchase another edition online and would send it to my mentor and friend, D. A. Powell, as gratitude for his never-ending patience and wisdom bestowed upon me and over my work.) I have also come by Thompson's first collection, *Poems*, as well as his posthumous *Red Book*, and have had the pleasure of reading and reading them over the years. All three collections mark different emo-tional velocities and subject matters—hewn with technical perfection and complex musical and language structures—that demonstrate and prove Thompson's excellence and significance to the poetry canon.

A Folio of Images
from the Collection of Philip Trower

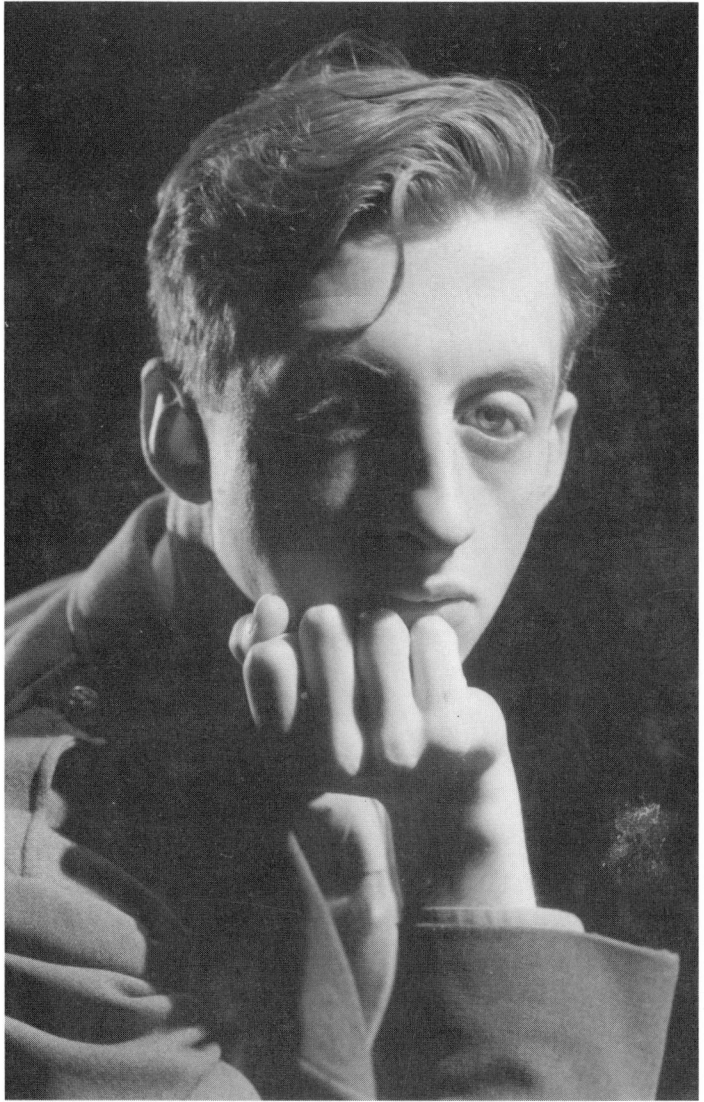

Dunstan Thompson, 1944-1945. Noted on reverse: "Taken by *Vogue*, I think in London, between the appearance of his first and second books."

Dunstan Thompson, June, 1945. Noted on reverse: "Taken by *Vogue* between the appearance of first two books, I think in London."

Dunstan Thompson, c. 1950.

With Philip Trower, Walsingham, c. mid-1950s

Walsingham, c. 1956

Undated drawing by Alfonso Ossorio

Clippings from *Vice Versa*

Volume I   10 cents   Number 1

VICE VERSA

November-December, 1940

FIRST AMERICAN ODE

TO RUSSELL SMART

Por que es justo que el hombre no busque su deleite
en la selva de sangre de la manana proxima.
Garcia Lorca

I

The skeleton of Lorca, shrieking like a horse,
    Gesticulates insanely from the forty-fourth story,
Warning me away, and the express contempt of Rilke
    Reduces the temperature whenever I remember;
Eliot uproots the one poem on the continent and
    Absconds with a copy of the Boston Evening Transcript:
The ghost of Poe haunts the poll booth, muttering,
    Begging a gin; tremendous from a typhoon
The voice of Herman Melville, pronouncing impossibles,
    Proves man is Jonah and the truth is god.

When I saw manhandled Manhattan gilding all meridians
    With Corinthian capitals, and the Neon
Investigating the domain of the swallow and the aeroplane,
    Then I recognised that category was ended:
The chaos is come of the organised disorder,
    The consistently inappropriate and the simple wrong:
I collect postcards of Hearst's palace and I hear
    The imitation Lincoln Senator roaring
Down theatrical corridors of Time and the Monroe Doctrine:
    Not the dialectic's opposite but chaos.

The first issue of *Vice Versa*, November-December, 1940

ENCYCLICAL

There are many reasons which may be offered for publishing this maga-
zine. Some are at once apparent. Obvious, of course, are the editors' per-
sonal reasons: the natural pleasure in proprietorship, the common desire for
self-publication. Beyond these are other closely related ones.

First of all, it is intended that this magazine shall be a means to attack
the smugness, the sterility, the death-in-life which disgrace the literary jour-
nals of America. Vilification and invective—weapons ancient and honorable
in our intellectual history—will be cruelly used upon those phantom figures
of diseased distinction who have for too long inhabited their over-stuffed
editorial chairs. Where all else fails, ridicule may hasten an unwarrantably
delayed departure. Academecians, ideologues, aesthetes, the whole worth-
less lot of those who sublimate their own artistic frustration by constipating
the publication and appreciation of their betters, must be cast into exterior
darkness where the wailing and gnashing of teeth may be an amusement to
the self-devils who torment them.

Secondly, this magazine does not propose to clean only one-half of the
Augean Stables. If the contemporary journals are bad because of their
editors, they are worse because of their contributors. Obscene old men,
whose reputations are no more than literary—derived from work done far
in the past, now vitiated by boredoms of obsessive writing, since they refuse
to die with decency, must be put away before their already corruptive mor-
tality becomes too nauseating to be endured. Nor should any mercy be ex-
pected by those in the fattening forties who, married to middle age, yet
still flirting with adolescence, lack both the achievements of maturity and
the promises of youth. As for the golden lads, whether they come with the
humous provinciality of the yokel, or the gas-light sophistication of the
slicker, they need not think that their sentimentalism, be it from the pig-sty
or the ballroom, shall escape the white light of truth that burns with the
fire of the phoenix. All, all of them, fakers, frauds, and counterfeits, all of
them must be destroyed.

In the third place, this magazine exists to publish good poetry. It will have
no room for cliques and claques of critical hacks. Whatever be the poet's
race, color, creed, or previous condition of servitude, the sole standard will
be whether his verse is publishable as *poetry*. The fashionable and the un-
known, the famous and the discredited, the ancient and the contemporary,
each of them will come naked to his judgment. Art is above temperament
and technique: it subtends infinites of worth. Hence, these pages will always
be open to the pure of heart.

Finally, this magazine represents the world of the present and the future.
It is in no sense a memorial to the past. It will conserve only those methods,
disciplines, traditions which have value for today, and will welcome only
those discoveries, improvisations, experiments which create tomorrow. It
will avoid both the sectarian and the eclectic. It will, as must anyone properly
conscious of the momentum of art, steer a middle way, escaping the rocks
of reaction and the whirlpools of anarchy. How difficult such a course will
be to maintain needs no elaboration. Nevertheless, that course is charted,
that voyage is begun. In so sailing, the magazine anticipates its enemies as
much as its friends. The presence of the former will be assurance that a fight
is fully joined. The existence of the latter will be proof that the battle holds
promies of more than passing victory.

D. T.

CUMMINGS IS A FINE PLACE TO GO FOR A VISIT,

BUT I WOULDN'T WANT TO LIVE THERE

50 Poems, by E. E. Cummings. New York: Duell, Sloan & Pearce. 73 pages. $5.00.

E. E. Cummings has written poems of great charm, even of great beauty. Such lyrics as "Somewhere I have never travelled," and "Since feeling is first," the latter with a conclusion almost Marvellian in its completeness, are beyond criticism, certainly beyond compare. Much of his light verse is equally delightful. One need only recall "Poem"—vitriol at Harold Vinal, or "The Cambridge Ladies"—deserved devastation. In his most recent book, *50 Poems*, both styles are represented: the one, simple, sensuous, and passionate (absolute definition); the other, wise, witty, and outrageous (approximate qualification). The collection is not only pleasant to look at— this limited edition is very handsome—but also charming to read.

Such, at least, is what one thinks on first finishing the poems. But later, and not so much later at that, one begins to wonder a little, to read again, even, finally, to challenge. For ultimately the conclusion is inescapable that this book is disappointing. After every merit has been recognized, every felicity approved, the result is still less than has been hopefully expected. It is like changing English banknotes into American currency: the pound, no longer worth five dollars, fluctuates instead around three. In large de- nominations, the loss is not slight. In reading 50 poems by Cummings, his failures are not unapparent.

Right away, it is best to dispose of the typography trick. At its most extreme—skewered syntax, garbled grammar, persiflagious print—the man- nerism is often successful. But as it is employed in so many of the poems, it is no more than a weak attempt to deck out a bad piece of work. In fact it is just as honest as the chromium extravanganza that passes for ad- vanced art in the decoration of bus terminals, cocktail bars, and the lobbies of theatrical hotels. The one justification for Cummings' obsession with typography is that, as understood by him, it serves as guide to emphasis when being read aloud—sense significance depends on pausing at every printer's symbol, which results, according to the theory, in comprehension similar to that given by the commas and semicolons in an extended periodic sentence. The only trouble with this is that it does not always work. Instead, like reading a language in which none of the irregular verbs are known, the sense of the page often becomes a matter of personal caprice. And, since the translation is obviously nonsense, one decides in the future to stick to English. The time is past when verse is modern by reason of its tricks, and important because it cannot be understood. Affectations that deliberately distort meaning and frustrate comprehension are sufficient sign that the poetry is not worth being read. One may, if one insists, call it chopped steak, but it is still hamburger.

Apart from the presentation of the verse, there are objections to be raised against it as poetry. To consider the lyrics first, one must admit that when Cummings fails to bring them off, the failure is emphatic with embarrassment. In this connection Swinburne's little gems about babies come to mind. One wishes that they had never been written. Likewise with Cummings, his complete lack of self-criticism tolerates in print verse that is more ridiculous, since unexcused by age, than the soul searchings of fifth formers at school. Lower case or not, whimsy-whamsy is bad on the eyes and hell on the appreciation. As for the dirty verse, for that after all is just what it is, fun is fun, but there are limits. Cummings is self-consciously unaware that they exist. More often than otherwise, one has the feeling that he is trying to compete with the anonymous troubadours who decorate the walls of public bathrooms. It is a losing game—there are some things that even the most enlightened publishers will not print. His rivals work under no such handicap. Yet he still produces the not-so-amusing-as-he-thinks versifications, and, of course, there are not wanting the peterpans whose unsurvived adolescence such delights inflame. For that matter, Cummings has a streak of permanent adolescence so deep that it often deserves the epithet "childish." Again, comes the unavoidable remembrance of Swinburne: elephantine eroticism.

And yet—for that, surely, is the way any condemnation of Cummings should conclude, and yet he is not, in the jargon of the academicians, wholly without merit. When all the clever, not quite accurate remarks have been painfully put into type, one is left with the realization that not more than a surface has been defaced. Against his scandalous disregard for the language must be set his fascinating usage of minor parts of speech. In this collection particularly, those stylistic orphans, articles, prepositions, and conjunctions are employed in a way to shame the average versifier who depends upon them for no more than metrical filler. At times, and there is no getting away from it, Cummings is as good a linguist as Joyce. When he is, the typography demands respect and, more important, attention. Moreover, here, as so often before, there are lyrics which make those by other names pale as stars before the moon. And there is one poem, "flotsam and jetsam," which is funny, though dirty, and, because dirty, true.

So, at length, one is where one started This new book is "charming," and

now the word is used in its most accurate sense. For all the aberrations of genius, Cummings writes poems that are poems. There are too few persons to contest such a distinction. Consequently, reading these 50 phantoms of delight, one is in the position of a visitor to a writer ancient with fame. One expects, even welcomes, the flashlight tour of the portrait gallery, the interminable reminiscence of Browning, and, of course, the ultimate signed edition. Because, when the occasion is over and one is busy phrasing it for cocktail conversation, the realization is unavoidable that what makes him worth describing is the fact that he *is* important.

DUNSTAN THOMPSON

From *Vice Versa* vol. 1, no. 1

AROUND THE TOWN

Oh, someday, my beauty, someday you'll be dead.
    No more Lilly Daché hats, no more Delman shoes;
    No Gunther furs to wear, no Bendel frocks to choose:
But there'll be the worms, there'll be the worms instead.
    No more Flato rings, no more orchids from Max Schling's;
    No Mercedes to drive, no Chanel Number Five:
For someday, my beauty, someday you'll be dead,
And there'll be the worms, there'll be the worms instead.

Oh, someday, my gallant, someday you'll be dead.
    No more suits from Brooks, no more jackets from J. Press;
    No Spaulding socks for sport, no Sulka shirts for dress:
But there'll be the worms, there'll be the worms instead.
    No more Cartier studs, no more handkerchiefs from Budd's;
    No Piper Cub to fly, no old Porcellian tie:
For someday, my gallant, someday you'll be dead,
And there'll be the worms, there'll be the worms instead.

Oh, someday, my darlings, someday you'll be dead.
    No more Tyson seats, no more Carnegie display;
    No paintings from Duveen, no books from Holliday:
But there'll be the worms, there'll be the worms instead.
    No more Tiffany blue box, no more Morgan stocks;
    No drinks at Twenty One, no El Morocco fun:
For someday, my darlings, someday you'll be dead,
And there'll be the worms, there'll be the worms instead.

                           M. D. TARANTULA

A poem by the probably pseudonymous M. D. Tarantula.
The true author is likely one of the editors of *Vice Versa*.
From vol. 1, nos. 3,4,5.

AVE FRATER ATQUE VALE

I am writing this on the third day of war. The future—not only for me but for this magazine—is utterly impossible to foresee. Harry Brown has already been drafted: is now a Corporal. I see no reason to believe that I shall not have military duties of my own very soon. The chance of the two of us being able to edit VICE VERSA from Singapore or Dakar is slight. As it stands at present, this issue would appear to be the last.

All of our contributors, subscribers, and happy-go-lucky readers are sufficiently aware how delayed the magazine has been in publication for me to dispense with tears and treacle statements about the "sad loss" to literature should we find it imperative to suspend appearance. The truth of the matter is that I am a bad editor—inefficient, dilatory, given to talk instead of action. Indeed I have such a fixed loathing for writing prose of any sort that what reviews I have written are the result of beer and—if I must say it—skittles rather than burning conviction: the phoenix fire of truth. Now that my colleague is no longer here to wake me early the langour has become obsessive. It is as much a miracle as a good poem that this issue is published. I am still startled by my ultimate energy.

With such an editorial situation it is no wonder that letters have not been answered, brilliant verse has gone unread, postcards demanding undelivered copies have been ignored. VICE VERSA was always an amateur affair—things were done when the spirit moved us. That may have its bad points. But the magazine was only valuable to us so long as it was fun to work on it. When it became a chore, I at least, was not amused. The chief reason, I think, that at times—particularly last summer—it was less than gayety to get VICE VERSA out was the extraordinary quality of the verse we received. To call it bad would unduly dignify it. Swill is the word I like. After weeks of reading little wonders, nausea began to be accustomed. Every tenth-rate versifier in the country favored us with his or her horrors. We ran out of rejection slips. In the meanwhile, the good poets with a few exceptions gave us praise without poems. Cummings, for example, did not answer letters: Stevens held out as yet unfulfilled hopes. Prokosch—to digress from the subject—was so annoyed by our rather mild review that a transatlantic holograph letter anathematized us for what he probably considers eternity. It is of course possible—as this issue shows—for us to fill a number of pages with our own works of genius. But that is not the only reason we began this magazine. Theoretically there are poets in this country whose work should glorify our publication. We thought that it would be pleasant to publish them along with ourselves and friends and enemies whom we thought worthy but unexploited. While I think that this number has its virtues, it must be said that less than a tenth of the verse was unsolicited—that much of it required heroic efforts (vide Pound) to secure. Since we are not professional editors, but rather, in our own opinion at least, poets, that state of affairs is intolerable. Better no magazine than one that is unpublished for six months because of its non existent contributors.

In order that those trusting charmers, our subscribers, should not feel that they had been "taken" for their fifty cents, I have made this a triple number. Some of the verse we have had for many months; other poems are of recent vintage. The reviews likewise vary—those by Brown were written last summer. The magazine as a whole I consider rather wonderful: all the verse is competent—some much more than that: the reviews should enrage a sufficient number of people to make them a success. Since we are now, I take it, allies of Great Britain, one hundred copies of this number will be offered for sale in London and the University towns. I hope that any British readers will not only enjoy us but will also keep us in their prayers.

I cannot assure *Poetry* that this is the final number of VICE VERSA. If a sufficiency of decent verse arrives before Easter, I shall do my best to bring out another issue then. Even if I have to wait longer, I shall still have hopes of more gayety in print. I see no real reason why spasmodic editions of the magazine should not appear for years to come. At any event the post office box will still be a good place to deposit those gems of genius.

Now at the turn of the year when the season of our fortune veers in the dead direction, I offer my thanks to all those who made this magazine possible. Particularly am I grateful to those poets who took a chance, to those first subscribers who acted from faith alone. To them and to everyone who wrote for us or read what others wrote, I wish Good Luck.

Not fare well,
But fare forward, voyagers.

DUNSTAN THOMPSON

From vol. 1, nos. 3,4,5, the last issue of *Vice Versa*

Revisiting *Vice Versa*
by Dana Gioia

Of all the literary scenes
Saddest this sight to me:
The graves of little magazines
Who died to make verse free.
—Keith Preston

It is impossible to tell the story of modern American poetry without examining the role of little magazines. During the twentieth century these idiosyncratic, mostly ephemeral, and inevitably uncommercial journals provided the one consistent home for poetry, poetics, and poetry criticism. While many poets published in large commercial magazines such as the *New Yorker* and *Atlantic*, the vast majority of modern verse appeared in journals with limited circulation edited by tiny staffs, often only one or two volunteers. These small magazines were not marginal to literary history. They did not publish only experimentalists and dissidents, nor did they serve mostly to discover promising young writers—although these journals fulfilled exactly those functions. By the middle of the twentieth century little magazines, published most new American poetry of every school and tendency—both mainstream and marginal. But their success came at a price. Although they achieved enormous literary influence, their readership remained small. While they succeeded in supporting poet-

---

Dana Gioia is a poet and critic. For six years he served as Chairman of the National Endowment for the Arts. His poetry collection, *Interrogations at Noon*, won the 2001 American Book Award.

ry, they also inadvertently helped compartmentalize it.

The great age of the little magazine has gradually come to an end as the internet has changed both the economics and sociology of poetry publication. Small magazines survive in vast numbers, but their role in literary culture has diminished. They remain important but are no longer unique in their role as an alternative to commercial publication. In retrospect, their great age roughly coincided with the twentieth century. The names of the leading small magazines still remain well known to most writers over forty—*Poetry*, *The Dial*, *The Partisan Review*, *The Hudson Review*, *The Fifties*, *Kayak*, *Yardbird Reader*, *Grand Street*. These were not only journals that published poets; they also trained them as editors and critics. In the days before blogs and websites, few serious poets failed to serve a stint as an editor or reader for a little magazine.

I must confess the pleasure I've taken in searching out and reading little magazines. In college when I should have been writing a paper or memorizing German verbs, I often spent hours looking through the bound issues of *Partisan Review*, *The Criterion*, or *Horizon*, dusty volumes that seemed to have long laid undisturbed in the stacks of the Stanford Library. Paging through the issues and reading poems, stories, essays, reviews, and editorials—sometimes just scanning the titles of works and names of contributors—gave me a tangible sense of a vanished cultural moment. For years I've also picked up copies at bookstores or through dealers. Although I can make a high-minded scholarly argument for these acquisitions, now shelved or copiously piled in my studio, my main motive has surely been the bibliophile's greedy pleasure of possession. Even the evocative names of many defunct but once lively journals still give me a small poetic frisson—*Blast!*, *Furioso*, *The Fugitive*, *Kulchur*, *Hound and Horn*, *Burning Deck*, *Sparrow*, *Botteghe Oscure*, and *Tiger's Eye*.

Vice Versa deserves a small but honorable place in the bustling history of American little magazines. Running for only three issues from November 1940 through January 1942, *Vice Versa* tried with unabashed ambition and exuberant irreverence to serve the classic function of the small magazine—to make a difference in the literary culture. Publishing only poetry and poetry criticism, editors Dunstan Thompson and Harry Brown, who had been contemporaries at Harvard, understood that to matter a little magazine had to make a big noise, and they announced their presence with the panache and self-assurance in which Harvard students have such alarming expertise.

Vice Versa did not espouse a particular poetic school or aesthetic. "Art is above temperament and technique," Thompson declared. The journal's program focused on literary excellence *per se*, and it displayed a broad view of what constituted good poetry. *Vice Versa* could publish W.H. Auden, Dylan Thomas, and Ezra Pound in successive issues accompanied by poets as dissimilar as Weldon Kees, Edith Sitwell, Conrad Aiken, George Barker, and Ivan Goll. If Thompson and Brown had a slight formalist bias, it was no more pronounced than in the *New Directions* annuals and Poet of the Month chapbooks published at the time by their Harvard acquaintance James Laughlin.

Modestly printed without a heavy stock cover, *Vice Versa* exuded the practical and austere tone of a reformist enterprise. There were no illustrations or artwork of any kind; the clean and balanced typography announced that careful language meant everything to this journal. Although contentiously independent, *Vice Versa* understood the importance of featuring well-known contributors, and each issue presented an impressive roster of talents, both established and emerging. Even seventy years later one recognizes most of the contributors, who not only included Auden, Pound, Thomas, Kees, Sitwell, Aiken, Barker, and

Goll, but also Richard Eberhart, Howard Nemerov, Nicholas Moore, John Malcolm Brinnin, Horace Gregory, Herbert Read, and Marya Zaturenska. They also published the work of Harvard's Pulitzer Prize-winning Boylston Professor, Robert Hillyer, who had taught Thompson, Brown, and Nemerov in Cambridge.

What gave *Vice Versa* its special character was a passionate conviction that poetry mattered. This conviction is everywhere apparent in the journal but nowhere expressed more vividly than in Thompson's flamboyant "Encyclical" in the first issue. To say that this statement of editorial mission is a classic little magazine manifesto understates its powerful concision and reformist zeal. The title, "Encyclical," was well chosen. Thompson's prose adopted the confident tone of an *ex cathedra* papal declaration: *Vice Versa* wasn't just a literary magazine; it represented an aesthetic crusade "to attack the smugness, the sterility, the death-in-life which disgrace the literary journals of America." If Thompson's savagely satiric tone now seems a bit too cocky and self-important, his clear and courageous statement of artistic principles still radiates a refreshing idealism. The literary manifesto is not a genre for the meek and self-questioning. Reform requires confidence and conviction.

When Thompson announced that no group or generation would be spared *Vice Versa*'s cleansing criticism, he was not striking an empty pose. The reviews that filled the back pages of *Vice Versa* were exceptionally exacting, even by the generally tough standards of the early Forties. *Vice Versa* did sometimes employ the vilification, invective, and ridicule Thompson threatened. Brown dismissed Carl Sandburg as a "tenth-rate, cheap-jack poet standing up and spouting vicious nonsense" and nicknamed editor George Dillon's *Poetry* "Mme. Dillon's Waxworks Museum." Edna St. Millay, "the Boadecea of Austerlitz," was Brown's particular *bête noire*. Judging her *Make Bright the Arrows*, he concluded, "The only word to describe this book is *sloppy*, though it's also childish, sentimental, irrational, and inane."

In his reviews Thompson offered more thoughtful and balanced but nonetheless often depreciating criticism. He rarely ridiculed or castigated his subjects, but he did place enormous demands on their works and usually demonstrated their failure to measure up. Thompson was particularly interesting on Wallace Stevens whom he called "certainly one of the best poets writing in America to-day," before adding the deflationary observation, "This statement is to be taken as a truism, not as a compliment. In fact, considering the present impoverishment of poetry, it is no compliment at all." Admiring the beauty of Stevens's poetry, he disliked its "chill impersonality." Likewise Thompson severely criticized E.E. Cummings but then went on to admire aspects of his work, and later reviewed W. H. Auden's *The Double Man* in mostly negative terms before selecting specific passages for praise. Reviewing books, Thompson did not assess them against other new volumes; he judged them against the canons of great literature.

Although informed, alert, and intelligent, Thompson was not a natural critic. He had no interest in ideas *per se*, and he was not drawn to the careful analysis that enlivens the work of the more gifted critics of the period such as R.P. Blackmur or Yvor Winters. Certainly in comparison to the New Critics, Thompson's criticism appears undisciplined and subjective. He rarely elaborated his ideas to explore them fully and offered no consistent theoretical basis for his judgments. For Thompson, poetry reviewing was primarily an exercise of taste—determining how good the new work was—rather than a job of analysis. Despite their limitations, his pieces in *Vice Versa* display the virtues of candor, intelligence, and conviction. They provide the reader of both his own time and today with a frank account of what one informed and careful writer of fine sensibility and broad taste thought (and felt) about the highly regarded poets of his time. If today this testimony seems bound by both personal and public history, Thompson's smart and colorful prose retains the authenticity of its cultural moment and the author's imaginative intelligence. And for admirers of Thompson's own verse, these early reviews provide the most extensive statements of his personal poetics.

Any discussion of *Vice Versa* would be inadequate that did not mention the mordant humor and youthful high spirits of the journal. (Thompson was only twenty-two and Brown twenty-three when *Vice Versa* first appeared.) The editors used satire, ridicule, and parody as critical weapons—as well as vehicles to display their wit. When George Dillon responded to *Vice Versa*'s attack on *Poetry*, Brown ended his rebuttal with mock courtesy:

> We won't mow the grass around his grave any more; it disturbs him too much. In fact, we're rather embarrassed to have aroused *Poetry* to an attack on us. It's like having a dead maiden aunt stand up in her coffin and do a jig.
>
> (from "Zombie")

Critical reviews and prose items bore titles like "Edna Makes the Supreme Sacrifice," "Look Out! There's a Modern Library Giant in that Cockpit," and "Pardon Me But Your Clay Feet are Showing." However sophisticated its vision, *Vice Versa* never lost its undergraduate irreverence.

Each issue also featured a satiric poem by M.D. Tarantula, which I assume—without external evidence—was a pseudonym for Thompson possibly in collaboration with Brown. The verse is too good to be by anyone without considerable talent:

You'd be a genius as a general.
  ("The art of war is to retreat.")
You'd be a wizard as a writer.
  ("Let me have that whiskey neat.")
            (from "Your Hit Parade")

Especially amusing were *Vice Versa*'s contributor's notes, which appeared only in the final issue. How could one resist a magazine written by poets described so memorably? Here are a few entries:

Weldon Kees—keeps bees.
Howard Nemerov—the nightclub singer; subscribes to the *Kenyon Review*.
Ezra Pound—a minor poet of the school of Cavalcanti; does propaganda work for the Italian regime.
Herbert Read—is a character in a book by Wyndham Lewis.
Dunstan Thompson—is sensitive, unspoilt, and thoroughly charming; lives on a barge in the East River.

That final issue dated January, 1942 also contained the announcement of *Vice Versa*'s dissolution. In a column titled "*Ave Frater, Atque Vale,*" Thompson announced:

I am writing this on the third day of the war. The future—not only for me but for this magazine—is utterly impossible to foresee. Harry Brown has already been drafted; is now a Corporal. I see no reason to believe that I shall not have military duties of my own very soon. As it stands, at present, this issue would appear to be our last.

Although Thompson expressed hope that his friend and Harvard classmate, William Abrahams, might continue the journal, the third *Vice Versa* was indeed the final number. Advertised as a triple issue, it ran eighty pages versus the earlier thirty-six-page format. The editors clearly felt the need to publish everything they had accepted to leave no manuscripts stranded. To reflect the increased size of the issue, they also raised the cover price from ten to twenty-five cents.

Facing military conscription and the dangers of war, Thompson made another change in editorial policy. Despite his refreshingly frank admission in his "Encyclical" that *Vice Versa* had been in part created out of "the common desire for self-publication," Thompson had published only one of his own poems in each of the first two issues. (This tally does not include the work of the mysterious Mr. Tarantula.) Now in the final number he offered "Eight Poems," the largest group published from any author in the magazine's short history. Such overt self-promotion by the young writer who personally subsidized the magazine could easily be criticized—if the work had not been so distinguished. Five of the poems would appear in his first volume *Poems* (1943), and the group contained some of the finest verse Thompson ever wrote, especially the sonnet "This loneliness for you is like the wound," which appeared here simply as "Poem." Ornate and feverishly lyric, these poems show the full realization of Thompson's early baroque style, which combined emotional intensity, sensuous imagery and an alternately evocative and frustrating obscurity. If Thompson was going off to meet the apocalypse, he had left a testament that he had indeed been a poet.

Neither Thompson nor Brown would edit another magazine. After the war Brown became a successful novelist, dramatist, and screenwriter. His novel, *A Walk in the Sun* (1944), was made into a film in 1945, and he moved to Hollywood to write the screenplays for such films as *Sands of Iwo Jima* (1949), *A Place in the Sun* (1951) for which he won an Oscar, and *Ocean's Eleven* (1960). He died in 1986. Thompson's subsequent literary career seemed less sustained and successful. By 1947 he had published the last of his three early volumes of verse. He wrote one well-received travel book, *The Phoenix in the Desert* (1951), and one novel, *The Dove with a Bough of Olive* (1954). Having settled in England, he then seemed to vanish as a writer. No other books in prose or verse appeared before his death in 1974. The passionate aesthete of the early poems appeared to have disappeared into middle-aged quiescence. But as the posthumous publication of his *Poems: 1950-1974* (1984) eventually revealed, Thompson continued writing, despite the indifference of editors and publishers, creating a mature style of spiritual depth and intensity. The idealist who wrote the "Encyclical" in the first *Vice Versa* had not misrepresented himself. To use his own editorial metaphor, he had begun the voyage and followed its difficult course faithfully to the end.

Battles in the Boudoir:
Thompson's Intimate Metaphors of War
by Heather Treseler

Dunstan Thompson's poetry challenges the ornithology of the critic, whereby poetic feather and flight pattern are assigned a school, a distinct niche within literary-historical time. Indeed, Thompson's recovery will require a shift and an expansion of the usual categories used to place mid-century Anglo-American poets, as his *sui generis* aesthetic necessarily revises the meaning of "war poet," "soldier verse," and "Middle Generation." Curiously like and unlike his American and British peers, Thompson was compared in the Forties to Dylan Thomas, W. H. Auden, Stephen Spender, and George Barker, but he remained somewhat of a lyric anomaly to his earliest reviewers—to Richard Chase in *Partisan Review,* Marian Castleman in *Poetry,* and H. P. Lazarus in *The Nation*—who struggled to reckon the complexity of Thompson's poetics and his half-closeted projections of homosexual desire.

Some critics heralded Thompson as the Second World War's avatar of the "Fated Boys" of the Great War who reinvented the war elegy in response to that cataclysm's unparalleled violence (Goldensohn 104). An editor for *The Commonweal,* for instance, wrote of Thompson in 1944:

Heather Treseler is currently a Presidential Fellow at the University of Notre Dame. In 2010-2011, she will be a Postdoctoral Fellow at the Academy of Arts and Sciences in Cambridge, Massachusetts, where she will be completing a book manuscript titled, *Lyric Letters: the American Epistolary Poem, 1945-1975.* Her critical work, memoirs and poems appear widely.

> Here is a living, speaking voice of youth enmeshed in war. We have not had one before, this time. Last time, we had Rupert Brooke. …[Thompson's] language is steeped with metaphors and usages and allusions which hold their most intense meaning only for a reader equally steeped in the central stream of Western culture.

Characterizing Thompson as the Brooke-like representative of his generation was multiply fitting: neither soldier-poet participated in combat and both drew upon erudition that would reward a learned readership. After his death in route to Gallipoli in 1915 Brooke was iconicized with the swan songs of pre-war British youth, whereas Thompson, though heralded in his hour, subsequently faded from recognition (Bergonzi 36). In Thompson's case, his belated Edwardian richness and obfuscation of forbidden desire may have unjustly consigned him to obscurity in his later years as sexual expression and a dystopian view of war became more poetically (and politically) *de rigueur.*[i] His oeuvre, now restored to circulation, is crucial to an understanding of Second World War poetry in its particularity and to a mapping of the postwar confluence of poetic styles that remade the American literary landscape after 1945. As a poet imitative of his predecessors but thoroughly engaged with the crises of the hour, Thompson exemplifies the hybridity available to an Anglo-American litterateur at the middle of the twentieth century.

While Thompson was responding to an Edwardian strain of modernism (one that included Housman, Brooke, and Monro), his early work also evinces the governing characteristic Steven Gould Axelrod locates in the "Middle Generation" of American poets born between 1910-1920: a conflation of the *oikia*, or themes of the household and interiority, with those of the *polis* or public sphere (2). It is a thematic integration that reflects this generation's position as the first to write after the death (and cultural apotheosis) of Freud and, more importantly, as the first to experience a global war with staggering civilian casualties. While 5 percent of the deaths incurred by the First World War were civilian, about 66 percent of the deaths in the Second World War were of private citizens and nearly 78 million people were killed or wounded (Bourke xxiii). The second war's broader involvement of non-combatants, its vast and disparate theaters, and its distinct ontological horrors—atomic warfare, genocide, and extensive aerial bombardment—have arguably made its historical (and poetic) legacy more heterogeneous, less easy to demarcate than the poetry of the Great War, which brought to bear the fact of *homo homini lupus est* so centrally and forcibly in Western consciousness.

The poetry of the Second World War, however, has often been read merely as a development of the first or, as Oscar Williams states in his anthology *The War Poets* (1945), with the understanding that "World War I was the opening *phase* of World War II" (8, emphasis added). This critical elision persisted for much of the twentieth century, impeding an adequate focus on mid-century war poets as a distinct literary generation. In his introduction to the international anthology *Second World War Poems* (2004), Hugh Haughton admits that the poetry of this conflict has long occupied the status of a "dead letter" beside the mythos of the "war poet" established by Great War legends like Wilfred Owen, Siegfried Sassoon, and Issac Rosenberg (xvii). With the retrospective distance of a half-century, the "letter" of Second World War poetry is a belated missive due for renewed critical receipt: recovering duly complex poetic voices like Thompson's will enable a finer apprehension of Second World War poetry in its specificity, and as one intrinsically linked (but markedly divergent from) the literary precedents of the Great War.[ii]

Thompson's war poetry should figure centrally in this unfolding legacy and deserves a place in any historicist or likewise comprehensive account of Second World War literature. His poems show the marks of his traditional schooling, including his study with the poet-critic Robert Hillyer, a Boylston Professor at Harvard University and a "gonfalonier of 'Reaction,'" who abjured the "restlessness" of Imagism for the gentlemanly verse of the sixteenth and late-nineteenth centuries (*Venture* 47; Hillyer 143). Adopting some of his mentor's predilections, Thompson also used his own experience of military service to describe the casual combat of relational life: the intimate contests of friends, foes, and lovers. Hence his poems share aspects of his American peers' biographic aesthetic (or the poem's seeming origin in actual experience), while they also wear a densely musical brocade akin to the Edwardian tones of Harold Monro, Rupert Brooke, John Drinkwater, and Robert Graves—poets whose aestheticized verse crested against the realities of the Great War like so many doomed "swimmers into cleanness leaping" (Brooke "Peace" 146).

Thompson's depictions of a largely *verboten* sexuality further complicate his stylized engagement with the themes of love and war. Although his military service as a corporal in the United States Army did not include combat, the tacit secret of his homosexuality, the war's strange wedding of thanatos and eros, and the spiritual dilemmas of his generation speak eloquently to our postmodern consciousness, wherein the persistence of warfare has become an interpolating presence alongside any *petit récit* of selfhood, friendship, or sexual desire (Lyotard 60). T. S. Eliot famously asserted in "Notes on War Poetry" that: "[It is] the abstract conception/ Of private experience at its greatest intensity/ Becoming universal, which we call 'poetry,'" and Thompson's verse occupies this liminal zone in which the private life of feeling acquires lyric currency (qtd. in

Houghton 68-69). In both *Poems* and *Lament for the Sleepwalker*, Thompson draws upon love's Pyrrhic triumphs to implicate the immediate context of war and the attendant complexities of the closet while reaching toward a "concrete universal" (Ransom 277). Hence in Thompson's best poems, the civilian reader can recognize himself—and the complications of desire—within warfare's hyperbolic enactment of human conflict.

One of Thompson's finer sonnets, "This Loneliness for You Is Like the Wound," compares the pain of an absent (or lost) lover to a mortal injury. The soldier, metaphorically rendered prostrate in a hospital bed, smiles bravely when the "general on his round" pins a "cross above/ The bullet-bearing heart" (*P* 35). After the soldier is "medalled," however, his body is almost instantaneously assailed by "Disaster" (*P* 35). As in Sappho's famous fragment thirty-one, the speaker feels each of his bodily systems fail as love-pain "[w]ins the last battle, takes the heights, and he/Succumbs before his reinforcements start" (*P* 35). Here the vocabulary of warfare, the semiotics of wounds, and the soldier's somatic battlefield intermingle within the musical elegance of a Shakespearean sonnet. But the poem also queries the legitimacy of these analogies: whether, during an era of total warfare, it is suspect to align the skirmishes of the boudoir with actual bloodshed, or lovers' cruelties with warfare's ravage of whole populations. Thompson concludes on an interrogative note that contains a tacit challenge: "Yet now, when death is not a metaphor,/ Who dares to say that love is like the war?" (*P* 35).

In many ways, Thompson distinguishes himself from other soldier-poets in that he does "dare[s] to say": he determinedly aligns the individual's battle-pocked quest for love with warfare's scale of human disaster. His presence in two popular wartime anthologies, *The War Poets* (1945) and *A Little Treasury of Modern Poetry, English and American* (1946), underscores the true heterogeneity of his style and the especial nature of his daring: Thompson extends the trope of soldiers' fraternity into an erotic dimension, staging this rhetorical risk alongside references to warfare's mortal dangers.

"Largo," a striking *ars poetica*, appears in both of these anthologies, which were edited by Thompson's influential friend Oscar Williams (whose skill as an anthologist thankfully outdid his own homage to the muse). A hundred and fifty-line poem, "Largo" reveals Thompson's coordinating influences as well as his major themes and characteristic registers. These include a blushing song-like quality that recalls Rupert Brooke; a variable diction that alternately echoes Shakespearean drama and Coleridge's conversation poems; and an amorous, valetudinarian despair akin to Keats's late, feverish letters to Fanny Brawne. Addressed to William Abrahams, Thompson's friend, fellow soldier-poet, and presumptive lover, "Largo" begins thus:

> Of those I have known, the few and fatal friends,
>> All were ambiguous, deceitful, not to trust:
>> But like attracts its like, no doubt; and mirrors must
>> Be faithful to the image that they see. Light bends
>>> Only the spectrum in the glass:
>>> Prime colors are the ones which pass
>>> The less distorted. Friendship ends
>> In hatred or in love, ambivalence of lust:
>>> Either, like Hamlet, haunted, doting on the least
>>> Reflection of remorse; or else, like Richard, lost
>>>> In vanity. The frozen hands
>>>> That hold the mirror make demands;
>>> And flexing fingers clutch the vision in a vice.
>>> Each one betrays himself: the ghostly glazier understands
>>>> Why he must work in ice. (*P* 9)

Both the glazier (or glass setter) working in "ice" and the poet working the high gloss of a verbalist's sheen are compelled to render the image of failed loves in a "faithful" mirror. The speaker's doomed view of human relation—the bitter end of all loves, platonic or erotic—rivals the economical lust in the "Fire Sermon" section of Eliot's "Waste Land," the calloused spectators of Icarus in Auden's "Musée des Beaux Arts," and the existential summons to fidelity at the end of Arnold's "Dover Beach." Referring to his "few and fatal friends," the speaker alludes to the potentially destructive turns in the exercise of affection or of possessive desire. Love is "[a]rmed," as the speaker later claims; at best, poets may serve as "cold-comfort guards" alongside its encampments (*P* 13).

Poised to begin a reconnaissance of betrayals and unhappy love affairs, the speaker gives himself this limiting premise: that the "lover" is likely to attract only his moral or spiritual equal. Hence any shortcoming that he locates in the character of a beloved is likely to reside in himself. By this formula, ardor is returned with the same narcissistic yearning (in the "mirror") and selfish desire ("clutch[ing] the vision") with which it is likely given. In the second stanza, however, the speaker upholds his lover as the exception to this misanthropic rule. Borrowing conceits from geometry and a royal court, the speaker intimates the furtive life of forbidden love, one carried out in a land where parallel lines can find a "meeting point.../... behind the backs/Of consort queens" (*P* 9). In Thompson's conceit, the demands of the State—the exacting decorum of the court—and of individuals' subversive desires dangerously coexist. This figurative circumstance is, of course, not unlike that of the homosexual soldier, falling in love with a coeval inside the authoritarian strictures of military life.

> All friends are false but you are true: the paradox
> Is perfect tense in present time, whose parallel

Extends to meeting point; where, more than friends, we fell
Together on the other side of love; where clocks
And mirrors were reversed to show
Ourselves as only we could know;
Where all the doors had secret locks
    With double keys; and where the sliding panel, well
    Concealed, gave us our exit through the palace wall.
    There we have come and gone: twin kings, who roam at will
        Behind the court, behind the backs
        Of consort queens, behind the racks
    On which their favorites lie who told them what to do.
    For every cupid with a garland round the throne still lacks
        The look I give to you. (*P* 9)

Thompson's prose rhythms are off-set by the sheer musicality of his lines: a dense pattern of rhyme and alliteration that sonically heightens his description of a clandestine, extra-legal liaison. Most of these lines (9 of 15) are also preemptively—and even protectively—punctuated with caesuras, as if to imitate the "doors" and "locks" within the stanza, the literal "room" of the poem. In this poetic space, the lover and beloved can travel the "parallel" of a "paradox" (love's truth) at "perfect tense in present time" (*P* 9). Defying normative rules, mathematical laws, and clock-time chronology, love is pitched against the expectations and the polity of the State.

The embattlement of eros with orthodoxy becomes quite explicit in several passages of "Largo"; this is a common trope in Second World War poetry, at least in a heterosexual context. To appreciate the daring in Thompson's expression of homosexual desire, it is helpful to remember that John Crowe Ransom, that New Critical titan of the postwar period, refused to print Robert Duncan's poetry in the *Kenyon Review* after Duncan published his essay, "The Homosexual and Society" in 1944 (Gunn 118). Yet Thompson's speaker bravely and plainly states that he and his addressee are indeed "more than friends," a couple who "fell/Together on the other side of love" (*P* 9). In an alternate, inverted world of "reversed" mirrors, "secret locks," and "double keys," they are at last able "to show/ Ourselves as only we could know" (*P* 9). Thompson emphasizes the necessary duplicity of this liaison: the speaker and addressee have escaped through a "sliding panel, well/Concealed [that] gave us our exit through a palace wall" (*P* 9). The pursuit of forbidden desires outside of the monarch's castle—outside of the official buildings of the State—is analogous to the hidden lives of gay soldiers, particularly those who would risk love within the jurisdiction of military life. Here "will" (in the Shakespearean sense of "carnal desire") must be "well" hidden inside the "walls" of sound-alike sound, and look-alike uniforms (OED 342).

According to Todorov, "transgression requires a law," and many of Thompson's poems invoke the "lawful" *polis* as they limn the dangers of physical passion (60). In "Largo," the speaker and addressee's trespass requires that they risk death: they love in defiance of the "consort queens" who torture on "racks" anyone who challenges their authority (*P* 9). It is in this atmosphere of perilous intrigue that the speaker asserts, unequivocally, the superiority of his feeling to the glib flattery of the queen's courtiers: "For every cupid with a garland round the throne still lacks/ The look I give to you" (*P* 9). Here sycophants' adoration of "the throne"—a disembodied symbol of power—is a mere charade beside the lover with evident designs upon his beloved.

Thompson's animation of courtly maquillage suggests the late Victorian/Edwardian influence of his collegiate mentor, Robert Hillyer, who famously kept a portrait of Queen Elizabeth above his desk at Harvard University, favored Bridges over Hopkins, and built several "Egyptian" rooms into his large home in Pomfret,

Connecticut (Thompson *Venture* 49-51). In his poetry handbook *First Principles of Verse* (1938), Hillyer explicitly legitimates poets' use of royalty or other "exalted" characters for dramatic effect:

> ... kings and queens are subject to all the human emotions and at the same time present a sufficiently exalted exterior to heighten our interest and sharpen our feelings for their doom. The contrast between their splendid trappings and their unhappy destiny brings into relief all the emotional values of tragedy. ... A parable or fairy tale will sometimes be more profoundly accurate than a day-to-day record of events in a mid-western suburb. (96-98)

Hillyer bridles against poets' use of the quotidian—the suburban fabric of many mid-century poets' lives—and the biographic aesthetic that the Middle Generation would bring fully into vogue in the 1950s. Thompson's poetry, however, reveals his ties to Hillyer's patrician fabulism and to his peers' aesthetic of historical verisimilitude. Hence, in "Largo" he utilizes the conceits of a royal palace; the antics of the Greeks and Trojans; the cruel games of Eros, "[a]n indolent and doubtful boy"; and the mute valor of Himalayan mountaineers. But his poetic narrative is most convincing when he addresses the fate of young soldiers caught in the death machinery of the current war.

Accordingly, the two stanzas of "Largo" that feature martial imagery have a weightier *gravitas* than the rest of the poem. In the sixth, Thompson describes the warring State's encroachment on private desires, a frequent leitmotif in Second World War poetry, but one to which he adds his own edge. The stanza begins startlingly, with the speaker's direct alliterative address:

> Make no mistake, my soldier. Listen: bugle calls
> Revoke your leisure like a leave, invade your peace
> With orders on the run, and, loud as bombs, police

Your life for death. The poet's blood-brick tower falls:
Even his vanity is gone,
Which leaves the loser all alone.
Not private poems, but public brawls
Demand his drumbeat history, the pulse that must increase
Until his heart is ransomed from its jewel. Revise
Your verse. Consider what kings' killer did to those
Who wrote their way between the shells
That last delusive time. Farewells
Are folly to our serpent queen. She will not sign
Discharge of conscience for a masterpiece, but, hissing, tells
Failure in every line. (*P* 11)

The speaker's monitory warning turns on five imperatives, progressively more threatening: "make," "[l]isten," "[r]evoke," "invade," and "police." These predatory predicates hunt the soldier for his "leisure," that linguistic cousin of "license": both of these words are derived from the Latin *licere*, meaning "to be permitted... [f]reedom to do something specified or implied" (OED 815-816; 890). Thompson's use of "leisure" hews closely to the word's etymological sense as not simply freedom from labor, but an unproscribed time and space, one which allows for the pursuit of pleasure, thought, and diversion. (Traditionally, leisure often connoted dalliance, as in these lines from Gower: "That she with him had a leiser/ To speke and telle of her desir" [OED 816].) Hence the root connotations of "leisure"— and of a soldier's likely activities on temporary leave—build upon the poem's atmosphere of innuendo such that "Largo" enacts the private sphere that the war-mongering State threatens to extinguish.

As Deborah Nelson has shown, privacy was a hotly fetishized and largely fictional circumstance in the postwar/Cold War period: a half-imaginary privilege that the lyric poem (alongside the private house, the car, and the telephone booth) was thought both to test and demonstrate (xiv). It would be another twenty years until, in

Griswold v. Connecticut (1965), American citizens' homes—
and bedrooms—were judged a constitutional "'zone of
privacy,'" but already, in the 1940s, Thompson was ardent-
ly protesting the State's conscription of "private poems,"
civic "leisure," and the heart's "jewel" (Nelson 68-71; 11).
Buffeted by "bugle calls," "orders," and "bombs," the sol-
dier-poet's life and artistic virility are duly threatened (*P* 11).
Indeed, the speaker reports watching helplessly as his phal-
lic "blood-brick tower falls," an event that cancels his "van-
ity" and "leaves the [war's] loser all alone" (*P* 11).
Encouraged to abandon the pathos of war, the soldier-poet
is asked to write a "drumbeat history" that will cause his
own pulse to "increase/Until his heart is ransomed from its
jewel" (*P* 11). Thompson figuratively truncates the warring
State to a bellicose rhythm, but one that threatens the sub-
tler *melopoeia* of the poet's visceral music. As Michael
Davidson has· noted, Thompson's contemporaries often
chose to represent public disorder in private ills: a Freudian
metonymy wherein unease in the body politic appears as
(mental or physical) disease in the individual (54).

The poet-speaker in Thompson's "Largo" is a prover-
bial canary in the coal mine of wartime coercion. Robbed
of his Yeatsian tower and of his lyric "leisure," the soldier-
poet must answer to "public brawls"—themselves the
germ of war—and with the patriotism that Pound deri-
sively called "Pindar's brass drum." Thompson strikes a
note of sardonic mimicry in advising William Abrahams,
his addressee (and fellow-soldier poet), to take up a jingo-
ist line: "Revise/Your verse. Consider what kings' killer did
to those/ Who wrote their way between the shells/ That
last delusive time" (*P* 11). Thompson also recalls the situa-
tion of the Great War poets, who presented the brutalities
of trench warfare against the policy of censorship and
rhetorical gloss pursued by most European governments
during that conflict. Here the disingenuous State appears in

the "serpent queen," a ruler who "will not sign/Discharge of conscience for a masterpiece" and who dismisses as a "[f]ailure" anyone who does not adhere to the energies of wartime mobilization, or the deadly sport of "public brawls" (*P* 11).

Thompson essentially juxtaposes the State's ultimate claims on soldiers' lives with poems' innermost privacies: the riddles of subjectivity, sexuality, ambition, and desire from which the lyric derives its animating grammar. He also acknowledges—and ultimately resists—the impersonalizing force of historical narrative or, to borrow from Auden, the superimposition of "public faces in private spaces" (54). This generative tension between the personal, symbolic story and the totalizing influence of meta-narratives is one that theorists from Lyotard to Nadel have identified as a mark of postmodernity and one that also serves to link Thompson, despite his stylistic differences, to some of his Middle Generation peers.

The individual's negotiation of selfhood in relation to the ontological shifts induced by war is likewise a theme in Thompson's prose. In his short story, "A Traveller to Deptford," (c. 1947-1948), the narrator attempts to deliver a bouquet of violets to the tomb of Christopher Marlowe. He arrives in Deptford and finds the church of Saint Nicholas abandoned, its adjacent graveyard disordered almost beyond recognition. Thwarted in his errand, the narrator broods on the war's generalizing affect—its theft of individuality, even that of a sixteen-century playwright, long adored. He states, "Now it did not matter much where the violets went; I could no longer honestly mean them for a private person; they were exacted by all these profaned dead" (*T* 141). Thompson insinuates that Marlowe's legacy has been at least temporarily disinterred with his grave: though a literary genius, he is now homogenized in England's elegy for all of its dead, all of its desecrated names. At this juncture, Thompson's story would appear to admit the conquest of brute history over any other rendering of human circumstance.

But his protagonist turns from Deptford to visit the Maritime Museum in Greenwich, a locale appropriate for investigating temporality's influence on subjectivity. Entering the museum, the narrator gives an epic catalogue of its contents, noting portraits of "murderous royalties, their attendant gangsters... the brutal butcher's face of the First Defender of the Faith and the bejewelled dispassion of the unsexed bastard queen called Gloriana" (*T* 143). Thompson's sardonic description of these royal thugs resonates with his disdain for the "consort queens" in "Largo" (*P* 9). Indeed when the narrator comes upon a gallery of imperial spoils, he offers this belittling condemnation:

> But there was more to see farther on and I dutifully saw it: sextants and quadrants and compasses and maps and astrolabes, miniature ships, miniature barges, miniature rowboats, gold plate and silver plate and commemorative crystal, chunks of the deck and bits off the bridge from various immortal dreadnoughts, memorabilia of heroes, their swords, their medals, their cocked hats, their brass buttons, and a whole pantheon of knickknacks and junk belonging to Lord Nelson, including a treasure chest of cheap presents given by him to Lady Hamilton. I looked at statues of sexless admirals, paintings of meaningless battles, the absolute deadness of history. (*T* 143)

In a passage of headlong parataxis, Thompson reduces the imperial glories of Britannia to nostalgic trinkets, toy-like miniatures, billet-doux, stolen goods, and the corpse or "absolute deadness of history" (*T* 143). This catalogue, moreover, visually rhymes with the graveyard scene in Deptford, wherein the stately rest of the dead has been grossly disturbed. Indeed, the anonymity of those buried in Deptford's graveyard contrasts with the Museum's secure homage to dubious heroes and debauched royalty. In the juxtaposition of these two *mise-en-scènes*, Thompson subtly links Britain's colonial hauteur to the devastation of the just-finished war. He also foregrounds the predicament of the literary artist, expected to serve the agenda of an empire that may well forget him.

In Thompson's poetry, there is one force duly resistant to historical erasure: that of passionate love. Only erotic ardor can defy the state's totalizing claims in many of Thompson's poems, and in ways that recall a piece of ancient graffiti that used to appear inside of the Jenney's Latin textbook: an acrostic in which *A-M-O-R* and *R-O-M-A* are spelled in an interlocking square. Thompson similarly presents a world in which love alone can rival the persuasive, terrific force of Roman *imperium*. The primacy that Thompson accords this rival "state" (with its two citizens, lover and beloved) is startlingly clear in the last stanza of "Largo." After nine symphonically woven strophes, the poet temporarily retires from conceit-making to cite his beloved's (unspoken, unwritten) name as the *locus in quo* of his own poetic voice:

> No marvelled metaphor avails
> To vantage his beloved impersonator twin,
> Whose coronet, crown crystal, qualifies a peer. My voice fails.
> In your name poems begin. (*P* 13)

As a dedicatory offering, these lines depict a generative surrender: they admit the fallacy of authorial singularity in the poet's dependency on a muse. Drawing back from the "marvelled metaphor," the speaker returns to the simplicity of a name: to a word that signifies the aura of the animating-Other (*P* 13). If we understand the poem's dedicatee and addressee to be William Abrahams, a fellow soldier-poet, then Thompson may be describing their own status as "twin kings," poets whose private demesne is threatened—and enlivened—by the greater historical contest in which they find themselves.

An eloquent defense of such mythologizing appears in T. Sturge Moore's classic volume, *Some Soldier Poets* (1920). In this modest anthology of Edwardian and Georgian figures implicated in the Great War, Moore defends some of the aesthetic principles relevant to Thompson's style: namely, a decorative mythological penchant that contrasts with the more "realistic" psychological verse of his Middle Generation contemporaries.[iii] Moore, for example, encourages the poet to boldly exalt his beloved: "If the poet treats of his own lover he must be careful not clearly to distinguish her from Helen of Troy, or should, at least, give us the illusion that they are equally real to him" (8). Shortly thereafter, Moore argues that "failure in love and war" will reward the poet more than success in either realm. Generous with his avuncular wisdom, Moore opines: "… when the real world [of love and war] has rejected a man he feels freer in the Muses' house; he no longer has any interests that conflict with theirs" (8). Thompson appears to have assimilated Moore's gospel: lost love and the spendthrift casualties of war animate the best of his poem-songs. His soldier-boys, true to Moore's notion, have the status of demi-gods or mythological heroes challenged by forces greater than themselves.

Thompson's "Nor Mars His Sword" evinces a mixture of this Edwardian myth-making and a Middle Generation emphasis on psychological interiority. Dedicated to Richard Hager, the poem recounts the experience of loving men who are subsequently fed to battle. Herein the fact of death—and of a "death-in-life" loss of passionate attachment—are provocatively elided. Initially, the speaker depicts himself as a veteran elegist, as one who has loved the "yellow haired/… [who] coin their eyes with money from my hand" in their journey to the underworld (*P* 21).

Death, in Thompson's narrative, appears to be the literal mother of beauty as these boys in their "good looks endeared/ To the rough boatmen, go, laughing, to a far land" (*P* 21). Resenting the dead in the innocence of their mirth, the speaker narrows his plaint in the second stanza to a remarkable entreaty (and rhetorical assault) of one particular lover—and perhaps of "Richard Hager," the addressee of the poem:

> You were the first—but may not be the last
> Contriver, O death-in-life long lover. Time
> Which we failed at school; time when devotions past
> Reason ransacked us—what moonlight for crime:
> That time runs out. Now I besiege a bad age
> With courage. And you in a wrecked square rage. (*P* 21)

An excoriating eloquence marks Thompson's sensual anger. Sets of semantic opposites ("first" and "last," "devotions" and "[r]eason") and internal rhymes (like "[c]ontriver" and "lover") give these six compressed lines an aural insistence, an adamant sound that is simultaneously off-set by an interrupting caesura in each line. Remembering occasions from school, from "devotions" pursued by moonlight, the narrator mourns the loss of all that pleasurably "ransacked" him and his addressee beyond the pale of law, beyond the bounds of "Reason." The concluding couplet, like a tombstone's epitaph, establishes the speaker and addressee in their newly fixed positions: the poet is left to "besiege a bad age" while Hager rests in the "wrecked square" of, presumably, a rough earthen grave.

With the retributive anger that often marks modern elegies, especially those of the Middle Generation, Thompson's speaker in "Nor Mars His Sword" accuses his addressee of robbing him of *amour propre*, that armor without which no soldier-poet should dare love's battlefield (Ramazani 4):

You turned me once against myself, and for
Your welfare I can offer nothing more.

At moments such as this my failure takes
Wing like the swan, and, singing, flies through death,
Air of the sad daredevil. (*P* 21)

Thompson provides the reader with a seasoned portrait of an imperfect but significant affair: a liaison thick with the exaltation, injury, and anguish of battle. It is as a soldier, scarred by this especial kind of war, that Thompson cordons his rhetorical sprezzatura into one of his more memorable images: "Tears, these snowflakes/ Mantle the ruined duchies underneath/ My eyes" (*P* 21). In an almost Christological gesture, the speaker offers his own visage as an authenticating text, one in which manifest physical suffering articulates his grief. "[R]uined duchies," moreover, conflate his physique with the defensible land of a kingdom. Presiding at the border of life-and-death like Christ in the agony of crucifixion, the speaker dramatically reappropriates a moment from Wilfred Owen's "Strange Meeting," that Great War poem famous for its assertion of the fraternity between embattled men, between foresworn enemies.

Patently phantasmagoric, Owen's poem suggests the true radicalism of Christianity (with its expressed edict of befriending one's enemy), but in a non-doctrinal context:

I am the enemy you killed, my friend.
I knew you in the dark: for so you frowned
Yesterday through me as you jabbed and killed.
I parried; but my hands were loath and cold.
Let us sleep now… (126)

Thompson's lines seem a deliberate mimicry of Owen's, although put to an altogether different philosophic and lyric purpose. Hailing his beloved as an "[a]ngel of anguish, [a] suicidal saint," Thompson defines an experience not of actual battle, per se, but of near-fatal love:

> I am your praising enemy, a faint
> Fellow, but the broken voice is still my own.
> Pray, rest—the world is wide awake. In heaven,
> I believe, even our deaths are forgiven. (*P* 21)

These poems conjure a conversation between the living and the dead and ultimately seek a peace denied to warring men. While both poets depict sociality (or love) concurrent with violence, Owen's speaker addresses his actual murderer, seeking some ultimate friendship over the arbitrary antagonism of the battlefield. Thompson, however, as a "praising enemy" (and a thoroughly modern elegist) memorializes love's intimate wounds in his repossessed but "broken" voice. Hence, while Owen's speaker invites his enemy to join him in "sleep," Thompson's speaker asserts an absolute boundary between those confined to "rest" and those left "wide awake." In Thompson's schema, the end of love has a permanence and a fixity as stern as death itself. Rapprochement is only possible in "heaven," that realm just beyond the linguistic or imaginative reach of the poem.

Thompson's reinvention of Owen's dramatis personae suggests the proximal, but distinct and establishing conditions for First World War and Second World War soldier-poetry. Poets of the Second World War inherited the Great War poets' legacy, one which had revealed trench warfare as an abattoir of youth, enlivening horrors otherwise disguised in governments' rhetoric of legitimation. Many Second World War poets, including Thompson, endeavored to bring the war even more intensely homeward: into the lives of non-combatants and into the emergent, Freudian rubric of understanding mass violence, genocide, and atomic destruction as inherent and universal forces in the human psyche. Thompson's poetry shares in the Middle Generation's portrayal of war as a pervasive psychological metaphor for the negotiations of friendship and love, those fraternal and erotic bonds classically thought to oppose—or to ameliorate—violent conflict.

A lyric minotaur, Thompson wrote as a belated Edwardian and a mid-century American, as a non-combatant and a soldier, as a psychological realist and as an aesthete. This admixture is generatively evident in one of his other, often-anthologized poems from the Forties: "In All the Argosy of Your Bright Hair" (*P* 22). The poem begins as a graveside elegy; its combination of Keatsian images ("argosy" appears, for example, in Keats' letters to Fanny Brawne), Shakespearean tenor, and homespun details mark the singularity of Thompson's style. The first lines are full of funereal keening:

> Whom I lay down for dead rises up in blood,
>   Drawn over water after me. His wavering
> Football echoes from the ocean floor. Blow,
> Ye winds, a roundabout. These bully sailors flood
> My eyes with tears, treacheries. (*P* 22)

The poet stumbles slightly here in his mixture of maritime and homely images; a "[f]ootball" sent up from the ocean floor seems, at best, a rather odd gift from Neptune and one strangely placed among watery "tears" and "treacheries." But by the second stanza, Thompson's "argosy" has been righted in its waters. The elegy proceeds in recounting the personal history of a love affair with the intensity and bravado of war reportage:

> When that damask duke took my heart for hound,
> I dogged him with praises, with poems, a beggar's homage.
> His blue eyes, fencing like a dance of swords,
> Ringed me from foemen, were night lights. I found
> He turned my head from death's entrancing image,

Gold in the desert sun, who sang: 'What words
You want, I have.' He saved me from my own hand
And the five assassins nervous for the grandstand. (*P* 22)

Thompson deploys complex imagery with remarkable compression: in eight lines, he evokes an affair that involved aspects of surrender and salvation, gross vulnerability and protection. Although the lover's "dogged" submission to his "damask duke" recalls Helena's abject solicitation of Demetrius in "A Midsummer Night's Dream," the beloved is credited for keeping his lover from suicide, from the fatal enchantment of thanatos.[iv]

Epic and profoundly Freudian contests of death and desire are fiercely enjambed in this poem. Nor are they extinguished, it seems, by the beloved's demise. Once the "soldier boy/ … goes after the goddess in the barbed-wire wood/ Who sells him secrets for a firing squad," the speaker becomes a listless widower (*P* 22). Walking the streets of the red-light district, he reckons a loss that has taken more than its pound of flesh: a grief that has induced sexual depletion or neurasthenia. Hence, when the unlovely "whores of Wardour Street, the Soho whores" ask the speaker for a "match," he cannot supply them (*P* 22). Shrugging off the prostitutes, the speaker opens the door of the "private" lyric to the breadth of a public entreaty, one hinged on his heartache:

Inside, the lamps are lit. If I should watch
       All autumn nights, I'd see no ghost. My light
Fingered friend stole the world away. Imperilled heirs,
You of the equal sadness, give him your prayers. (*P* 22)

Punning on the Homeric epithet of "rosy-fingered dawn," the speaker recalls both his lover's illuminating presence and his gentle touch. And, in a gesture characteristic of Middle Generation poetry, the poem's last line turns the history of an intimacy outward: the speaker asks for others' "prayers," those statements akin to poems in conveying with formal urgency the dearest wish.

Thompson sets the joys and sorrows of the boudoir next to the hyperbolic enticements and cruelties of warfare, suggesting that battle can mark the closest of human relations. Other midcentury poets, confronted with two world wars, would arrive at somewhat different conclusions. In "Man and Bottle" (1942) Wallace Stevens wagers that modern man must "find out what will suffice" in order to reckon war's barbarism. He warns, however, that such an inquiry will necessarily "destroy/Romantic tenements of rose and ice" (238-239). Thompson's poems are unusual in that they answer Stevens's edict to locate "what will suffice" while obstinately refusing to quit their "Romantic tenements." His uniquely mobilized Negative Capability allows him to consider mass homicide alongside the very drawing rooms, barrooms, military encampments and canteens in which courtship—or the shadowy, ad hoc rituals of eros—take place.

Many of Thompson's Middle Generation contemporaries would subsequently turn from the extremity of the Second World War to celebrate the postwar's reprieve of suburban prosperity. But in Thompson's oeuvre passionate attachment is never securely housed in a split-level home, with all of its heteronormative associations. Royal castles, battle encampments, military hospitals, and fantastic realms are instead his poems' domain. The titling poem of his second collection, "Lament for the Sleepwalker," features the speaker's heart as a predatory cat, prowling the outdoors for the figurative carrion of an erotic connection. The poem begins in dramatic apostrophe:

> The lion is like him and the elusive leopard:
> Nine lived, he ranges—killer cat—my heart.

Green is the hanging moss, and green the jungle
Creeper: green where the gold plantations part
Their bamboo branches for a murderer's head.
In green courts he eats meat from the green dead.

...

                                        Beneath
Lascivious fur, his regal muscles flex,
Digesting fire, the marrow root of sex. (*L* 1)

Thompson's backdrop is alternately worthy of the
Windsor palace or an equatorial jungle. This ambience and
the figure of the "killer cat" enable the poet to depict sex-
ual appetite without specific reference to gender or human
circumstance, although Thompson's "killer cat" eats of the
"green dead" or, perhaps, of the youth readied for war (*L*
1). Embodying the paradox of love and death,
Thompson's somnambulist feline is one of his more strik-
ing and outré creatures, and one that enlivens the very
deathliness of desire.

Among law-breaking monarchs and libidinal jungle
cats, the poet could intimate a verboten form of sexuali-
ty, albeit in high masquerade. Thompson's royal cat lives
in a world of Edwardian fancy that had haunted his imag-
ination at least since his collegiate days. Indeed, a lion
appears in Thompson's work nearly ten years before
Lament for the Sleepwalker in his profile of Isabella Stewart
Gardner, "The Lady and the Lion" (1938). In the way that
a biographical sketch can reflect the biographer in the
recessed mirrors of its prose, Thompson's own predilec-
tions appear in his admiration of Gardner's "career of
eccentricity" (*LL* 6). He describes how Isabella Stewart,
the daughter of a New York candy-merchant, acquired a
second fortune in her marriage to Jack Gardner and put
this wealth to extraordinary ends (*LL* 5). Defying the
Mayflower snobberies of her Bostonian peers, Gardner

pursued a reputation as a beguiling daredevil and a patron of the arts. Hence she cultivated a salon that included Henry James, John Singer Sargent, and James McNeil Whistler and invited members of the symphony orchestra to play in her home (*LL* 7). She was also notorious, however, for bathing in the Dead Sea; for building a Venetian palace in Boston's Fenway; and, as Thompson particularly notes, for walking a leashed lion down Tremont Street, a busy thoroughfare in Boston (*LL* 7).

With a variety of Gardner-like puissance, Dunstan Thompson built his own Edwardian palace of "damask duke[s]" and "twin kings" in the crux of his century's second seizure of global violence (*P* 22, 9). While his decorous aesthetic would seem to refuse the structuring claims of history, Thompson's poems evince a generational and cultural consciousness particular to the Second World War in revealing barbaric cruelty within the most intimate realms of desire and wish. In walking his "lion... and the elusive leopard" of non-idealized and homosexual love down the mid-century's narrowed streets of respectability, Thompson wrote as a well-disguised Jacobin within the Anglo-American aristocracy. But it is not simply for artistic courage that Thompson's work deserves thorough reconsideration. A reconnaissance of his poetics and their place in the landscape of postwar lyricism will quicken our belated sense of this generation's legacy, a timely assessment as we too look for what might suffice in an era of seemingly endless war.

Works Cited

Auden, W. H. *Collected Poems*. Ed. Edward Mendelson. New York: Random House, 1991.

Axelrod, Stephen Gould. "The Middle Generation and WWII, Jarrell, Shapiro, Brooks, Bishop, Lowell." *War, Literature, and the Arts* 11:1. (1999): 1-41.

Bergonzi, B. *Heroes' Twilight: A Study of the Literature of the Great War*. Manchester: Carcanet, 1996.

Bourke, Joanna. *The Second World War: A People's History*. London: Oxford U. P., 2001.

Brooke, Rupert. *The Collected Poems*. London: Sidgwick & Jackson, 1960.

The Commonweal, "The Young Men Go to War." January (1944).

Davidson, Michael. *Guys Like Us: Citing Masculinity in Cold War Poetics*. Chicago: U. of Chicago P., 2004.

Goldensohn, Lorrie. *Dismantling Glory, Twentieth-Century Soldier Poetry*. New York: Columbia U. P., 2003.

Gunn, Thomas. *The Occasions of Poetry, Essays in Criticism and Autobiography*. San Francisco: North Point P, 1985.

Hillyer, Robert. *First Principles of Verse*. Boston: Writer Inc., 1938.

Houghton, Hugh, ed. *Second World War Poems*. London: Faber and Faber, 2004.

Lyotard, Jean-Francois. *The Postmodern Condition: A Report on Knowledge*. Trans. Geoff Bennington and Brian Massumi. Minneapolis: U. of Minnesota P, 1993.

Millard, Kenneth. *Edwardian Poetry*. Oxford: Clarendon Press, 1991.

Moore, Sturge T. *Some Soldier Poets*. Freeport: Books for Libraries, 1968.

Nelson, Deborah. *Pursuing Privacy in Cold War America.* New York: Columbia U. P., 2002.

Owen, Wilfred. *The Poems of Wilfred Owen.* Ed. Jon Stallworthy. New York: W. W. Norton, 1986.

Ramazani, Jahan. *Poetry of Mourning, the Modern Elegy from Hardy to Heaney.* Chicago: U. Chicago P., 1994.

Ransom, John Crowe. "The Concrete Universal: Observations on the Understanding of Poetry, I." *Selected Essays of John Crowe Ransom.* Eds. Thomas Young and John Hindle. Baton Rouge: Louisiana State U. P., 1984.

Schweik, Susan. *A Gulf So Deeply Cut, American Women Poets and the Second World War.* Madison: U. of Wisconsin, 1991.

Shakespeare, William. *The Complete Works.* Eds. Wells and Taylor. Oxford: Clarendon P, 2005.

Stevens, Wallace. *The Collected Poems.* New York: Knopf, 1999.

Thompson, Dunstan. *The Lady and the Lion.* Spring (1938).

——- *Lament for the Sleepwalker.* New York: Dodd, Mead & Co., 1947.

——- *Poems.* London: Camelot P. Ltd., 1943.

——- "A Traveller to Deptford." *New Writing and Daylight.* Ed. John Lehmanns. (c. 1947-1948).

——- untitled memoir of Robert Hillyer. *Venture,* May (1962).

Todorov, Tzvetan. *Genres in Discourse.*Cambridge: Cambridge U. P., 1990.

Williams, Oscar. *A Little Treasury of Modern Verse, British and American.* New York: Charles Scribner's Sons, 1946.

——-. *The War Poets, An Anthology of the War Poetry of the 20th Century.* New York: John Day Co., 1945.

Notes

[i] In *Edwardian Poetry* (1991), Kenneth Millard defines "Edwardian" as a literary attitude of "counter-decadence," or a preservationist's regard for a cultural legacy thought to be decadently endangered, and an abiding fealty to Victorian and pastoral imagery (2-4). Millard historicizes the term "Edwardian" in the sense that it is used here: as a designation that necessarily extends beyond the strict dates of Edward VII's reign (1901-1910) and one that would include such figures as A. E. Houseman, Edward Thomas, John Masefield, Rupert Brooke, and Robert Graves, among others. "Edwardian" seems a more accurate characterization of Thompson than the over-generalized "Georgian" title, as this latter group minimally includes the forty poets featured in Henry Monro's six "Georgian" anthologies published between 1911-1922. As a belated Edwardian with particular debts to Houseman and Brooke, Thompson evinces an elegiac regard for a fading social order, an interest in Greek and Roman antiquity, and a keen attunement to the musicality of rhyme and meter. This stylistic orientation may have had as much to do with Thompson's class background— or what Philip Trower terms "the well-brought-up, well-mannered Dunstan of Aunt Leita's world"— as it did the tutelage of Robert Hillyer, an American poet with enduring loyalties to the late Victorian/Edwardian era, who taught Thompson for two years at Harvard University.

[ii] Haughton's choice of the letter is an apropos metaphor for Second World War poetry, as the letter was essentially the technology of relationship between the home front and the fighting fronts during the war years. The "scene" of the war letter being sent or received was also one of the most common wartime/postwar tropes in mass culture, and one which served to dramatize the war's polarization of gender roles (Schweik 86). The extent to which the personal letter was a model for the lyric poem itself is suggested by the appearance of epistolary tropes in mid-century American poetry and by its frequent appearance in postwar critics' descriptions of the then-contemporary lyric. For example, in his introduction to *A Little Treasury of Modern Poetry, English and American* (1946), Oscar Williams references the "private letter" as a measure of the lyric poem's efficacy: "[although] published poetry does not have the same latitude as a private letter... it is always better when it is strictly truthful" (5). Williams's emphasis on the "truthful" nature of the poem implicates the new kind of

verisimilitude that the two world wars enlivened in poetry, a biographic quality that the personal letter was thought to exemplify.

iii Moore includes Julian Grenfell, Rupert Brooke, R. E. Vernède, Charles Hamilton Sorley, Francis Ledwidge, Edward Thomas, F. W. Harvey, Richard Aldington, and Alan Seeger in his anthology. Quite noticeably, Wilfred Owen, Siegfried Sassoon and other soldier-poets who largely transcended (or ironized) Edwardian tropes in depicting warfare's brutality receive less than a chapter's notice in Moore's volume.

iv In Act II, Scene I of Shakespeare's play, Helena prostrates herself before Demetrius with these obsequious lines:

And even for that do I love you the more.
I am your spaniel and, Demetrius,
The more you beat me I will fawn on you.
Use me but as your spaniel: spurn me, strike me,
Neglect me, lose me; only give me leave,
Unworthy as I am, to follow you.
What worser place can I beg in your love—
And yet a place of high respect with me—
Than to be used as you use your dog? (l. 202-210)

Dunstan Thompson's "Beautiful and Butcher Beast" Unleashed and on the Prowl
by Jim Elledge

butch, butcher, butchest

I discovered the poetry of Dunstan Thompson when I read Joseph Cady's "American Literature: Gay Male, 1900-1969."[i] I was intrigued by what Cady said about Thompson, a simple, to-the-point statement:

> In two books of war lyrics, the now-forgotten Dunstan Thompson (1918-1975) made his homosexuality as manifest as he could given his intricate and dense style—the 1943 *Poems*, where "gay" is used wittily throughout (for example, "Images of Disaster"), and the 1947 *Lament for the Sleepwalker* (for example, "This Tall Horseman, My Young Man of Mars," "In All the Argosy of Your Bright Hair," "Nor Mars His Sword," "The Everlasting Gunman") (Cady 34).

It was Cady's phrase "intricate and dense style," and the list of extraordinary titles, that grabbed my attention, that invited me to find and read *Poems* and *Lament for the Sleepwalker*, which became the focus of this and another essay I've written about Thompson.[ii]

It was a little too late in my career to be directly influenced by Thompson's poetics. To a very large extent, my prosody was by then already set. Yet, when I first opened his debut collection, *Poems*, and then shortly thereafter, when I found and read his second and, to my way of

Jim Elledge is the author of many books, among them *A History of My Tattoo* (Stonewall, 2006), winner of the Lambda Literary Award and finalist for the Thom Gunn Award, and *H*, forthcoming from Busman's Holiday Press.

thinking, better volume, *Lament for the Sleepwalker*, I was immediately convinced I was in the presence of a kindred soul, one as obsessed by language—by the word and its palette of connotation and denotation, by its dance of cadence and meter, by its symphony of rhymes: internal and end-of-line; ear, eye, and slant—as I am. That he constructed his poems with Faulknerian sentences, those that range from the first line of the poem and careen line after line toward its conclusion, and that he obviously owed allegiance to Gerard Manly Hopkins, a poet who looms large in my personal pantheon of poets, attracted me enormously because Faulkner's sentences are a roller-coaster ride of cadence, a technique I love as much as a reader of a text as I do as the writer of one, and because Hopkins' sprung rhythm—that lovely explosion that happens when words collide, one against the other—is so present in Thompson's work as I aim for it to be in my own—albeit far more subtly.

What also helped to spur my interest in Thompson's art was the fact of his being what is so often called a "war poet." For several decades, I'd been intrigued by the war poetry of poets such as Wilfred Owen and how a subtle homoeroticism permeates so much of it. I'd been captivated by the fact that they so often expressed desire and "pity" (one of Owen's signature words, one easily misunderstood) toward other men simultaneously, the pity they felt meant to disguise the desire they also felt. I'd always believe that the pity/desire combination had everything to do with the war poets' closeted lives, that the "pity" was meant to camouflage their desire for their (usually) straight audience or, somehow, their desire actually was handicapped by the closet and may have been expressed as "pity," not as "love" or even as "lust."

Owen and his cronies—all English, all World War I commissioned officers, all products of the public school system, and all Brahmin in their background or, at the very least, in their worldview—approached the narrator and his beloved clinically. In fact, Owen anesthetizes his desire, never directly articulating it. He numbs his heart so that what he feels—and labels "pity," "sorrow," or related words that are so safe that one man may use them toward another without fear of retribution—isn't *really* what he feels at all.

Such is the problem I've always had with the typical "war poet." Too often he focuses entirely on "pity" or "sorrow," the only emotions Owen's narrator allows himself to express about another solider who, more often than not, is wounded: most certainly physically but also (and often) mentally. The amputee as well as the shell-shocked are the focus of his "pity" and "sorrow," which then direct the reader to the wrecked carcass that the narrator once desired. The typical war poet aborts desire when the body is no longer lithe, when the muscles are limpid, and when a death rattle—not the groan of orgasm—echoes in the trenches.

However, the American, World War II poet Thompson took a different stance vis-à-vis his poems' narrator and the object of his narrator's desire, between the lover and his beloved. He staged same-sex love, instead of disguising it with codes as others had done before him. Despite his overt dealings with homosexuality, he nevertheless protected himself from backlash through an easily-constructed yet highly-successful strategy.

Thompson's strategy was twofold, and it's apparent as underpinning for his *Poems* and for *Lament for the Sleepwalker*. First, he addressed two readerships—one gay, the other straight—simultaneously, offering the same text to each, a text that made sense to both at the same time. Thompson's embrace of *ambiguity*, in William Empson's sense of the word, is the siren song that finally drew me deeply into his poetry.[iii] His narrator desires men. He loves men. His poetry is adamant about it, but that fact is often missed by those unwilling or unable to read it on two levels at once or by those who simply are unaware that a text might—or should—be read two ways at once, with both making sense.

Instances of this strategy are many, and the following two examples, one from each of Thompson's two war volumes, reveal how subtle his strategy is. In the first example, taken from "Largo"—

you and I,
Who with the butchered ghost must stalk the battlements,
Shall watch—cold-comfort guards—how lonely lie the tents
Where strangers sleep together just before they die

—men "sleep together," a statement that's not simply about bivouacing, but also one about sexual goings-on between men. To "sleep together" is, after all, a euphemism applied to gays' sexual activities as well as to straights'. In a later poem, "In All the Argosy of Your Bright Hair," Thompson's strategy allows us to read "These bully sailors flood / My eyes with tears" also in two distinctly different ways. The first depends on our reading *bully* as President Theodore Roosevelt's favorite adjective, meaning "good," "wonderful," etc., and so we consider the line a moment of lamentation: the deaths, the bravery, the activities of the wonderful sailors bring tears to the narrator's eyes in thanksgiving and in acknowledgment of their sacrifice. Thompson—like his readers in the 1940s and early 1950s—would've known the popular president's favorite word, *bully*. However, *bully* also refers to "tormentors," "intimidators," etc., and with that definition in mind, readers understand the sailors also as persecutors or tormentors who attack him, causing pain or, perhaps, even as role-players who take on the sadistic role to the narrator's masochistic one, bringing tears of pain that are, to him, also tears of satisfaction. Certainly at the time in which "In All the Argosy of Your Bright Hair" appeared, most readers would have read the lines in the first way, as a sentimental and patriotic statement, but just as assuredly, a gay reader would have been aware of the overtones that accompany it.

Second, Thompson scripted his narrator's desire in long, complicated sentences that distract readers from its homoeroticism, serving as camouflage. In maneuvering through the compound-complex sentences that are also rich in image and metaphor and chock-full of wordplay, readers often don't recognize the poetry's homoeroticism. They get caught up in paraphrasing the passages and in translating the figurative language, the symbols, and the allusions into a simpler, more accessible "prose-sense" of the poems, and so he has diverted their attention. Those able or willing or savvy enough to negotiate Thompson's "intricate and dense style" witness his paean to—or condemnation of—his beloved firsthand, which we can see in "Largo":

> Narcissus, doubled in the melting mirror, smiles
> To see himself outfaced by tears, and, sorrowing, hands
> His ace of love to harlequin of hearts, who stands
> The distant edge of laughter. Time's joker still compiles
> Trick score of triumph, trumps the queen
> To play his knave of emeralds. Green
> Gamester reflects the water guiles
> Of palming, reads the gambled cards, and then demands
> Another pack to shuffle. But the glass partner bends
> The fate five fingers round a saint's stigmata, wounds
> By dealing diamonds from his nails.
> No marveled metaphor avails
> To vantage this beloved impersonator twin,
> Who's coronet, crown crystal, qualifies a peer. My voice fails.
> In your name poems begin.

Thompson is far more open in his view of the beloved than the times typically allowed, all too aware of the pros and cons of surrendering himself to another especially during times of war, all too aware of how any relationship with another soldier would, by necessity, be temporary. After all, the lover and his beloved are warriors whose very lives depend on their being focused on surviving battles and on killing others. *Survival*, that lovely euphemism for putting oneself first and others later, allows for carefree couplings—tricks, one-night stands—and for disregarding a sex-mate's feelings after orgasm. To be honest, survival is vital for any warrior on or even near the battlefield. After all, it would be foolhardy for a solider to fantasize about last night's bunk buddy while today he's dodging bullets.

Time and time again, Thompson's narrator pictures his beloved in contradictory and in decidedly unsympathetic terms, and it is his willingness to present the beloved in realistic terms that, finally and forever, hooked me. The lover offers his beloved neither "pity" nor "sorrow," per se. Instead, writing some three decades after Owen, Thompson allows his narrator to observe his beloved unflinchingly, with a cold stare. In "Tarquin," for example, we note that

> The red-haired robber in the ravished bed
> Is doomsday driven, and averts his head,
> Turning to spurn the spoiled subjected body,
> That, lately lying altar for his ardor,
> Uncandled, scandalizes him, afraid he
> Has lost his lifetime in a moment's murder:
> He is the sinner who is saint instead:
> This dark night makes him wish that he were dead.

Thompson-the-poet and Thompson-the-warrior recognized that soldiers must be realistic about their situations and succinctly states that fact in "This Loneliness for You Is Like the Wound": "now, when death is not a metaphor, / Who dares to say that love is like the war?"

Nor does Thompson's narrator romanticize where and how he meets at least some of the men in his life. In "Dreams of the Barracks Emperor," he admits he meets them while on leave, cruising the street. Each time, the couple hurries off to a nearby park or garden, where they have sex: "I walked the streets, a stage star hearing cheers / From blackout boys, whose lucent cats' eyes—in the garden / Later at leave-taking—ran me through like shears." He meets another, in this case a hustler, walking through an area well-known in those days as a haunt for male prostitutes—"a Times Square tout: / His smile mints money" ("The Point of No Return")—and he picks up another hustler in a bar: "the lurid gin / Palace, where lust and money collide / By the bar, then couple" ("Songs of the Soldier").

Regardless, he finds most of his sex partners among those with whom he's stationed, among the "secret convoy" of "Hyd, Absolon, Thy Gilte Tresses Clere":

> The question never finds an answer: boys
> Who take to talking take to drink as well';
> And I, rejected now by heroes, write
> My name like mist around the secret convoys
> Of those I love, whose dogwatch kept, still tell
> Glass beads for one another through the night.
>
> You too are one of them.

In fact, the narrator of "A Knight of Ghosts and Shadows," suggests what is apparent from reading the poems, that sailors hold a special attraction for him:

> all my sailing lovers come
> To grief, cry up a violent sea, wraith-tossed

Unlucky sea, the sea whose lustrous ghost
Glides through the central blue, your eyes.

Through it all, Thompson's narrator ultimately sees his couplings in a negative light. Momentarily exhilarating even initially satisfying, the love they share is always short-lived, as he reveals in "Images of Disaster"—"Now every meeting means a new farewell"—and ends in a destruction that may be metaphoric or real, as in "Articles of War"—"The boy who brought me beauty brought me death"—or as in "This Tall Horseman, My Young Man of Mars:" "This tall horseman, my young man of Mars, / Scatters the gold dust from his hair, and takes / Me to pieces like a gun." They never really ever result in what the narrator most desires—

> the devil, good-looking as a movie star,
> Moves among us, conversing his clever lies
> Over music and drinks and pleasure, at war
> With what we want most

—because neither the lover nor his beloved is in control of the situation. Rather, it's "the devil, good-looking as a movie star," a figure representing that bugaboo reality, who orchestrates their lives and their loves. Only in heaven, which represents the dream, the ideal, or "what we want most," the narrator tells us, "no one is lonely, where by your side / Stands the lover of ever you—there the two / Completely one celebrate the state of the sun" ("Leave Pride to Those Who Have Already Died").

What Thompson's narrator wants is never what he gets, as he reveals in "Largo:"

> What we have always wanted, never had, the ease,
> The fame of athletes, such happy heroes at a game,
> Beloved by every likely lad, is not the same
> As what we have: these measured methods how to please

An indolent and doubtful boy,
Who plays at darts, breaks for a toy
The sometime valued heart.

In the same poem, the narrator reveals an important fact about his "friends," a word he often uses for "lovers":

Of those whom I have known, the few and fatal friends,
All were ambiguous deceitful, not to trust…

. . .

Friendship ends
In hatred or in love, ambivalence of lust:
Either, like Hamlet, haunted, doting on the least
Reflection of remorse; or else, like Richard, lost
In vanity.

Still, in "The Return of the Hero," he wants to believe in friendship and in the possibility of finding love:

If friendship were fake—which the poet affirmed and denied,
While he went from one bed to another in search of himself,
Until for the last time, or was it the first, he woke up the dead
To tell them "I've fallen in love," and half joking, half
Serious, sang them to sleep again.…

While he's wont to believe that "all lust [is] a kind of love" ("Jack of Hearts"), he's just as clear that lust is, after all, simply lust despite his penchant for trying to make it more than that. It's easy to imagine him wincing at the realization that, for the "sad / Faced, grave eyed, beautiful as steel // Young man," whom he adores, he's little more than a "place of rest" ("Songs of the Soldier") for a few hours during shore leave as the chaos of war rages. In fact, although he seems sometimes to have gotten something positive out of his relationships, far too often, his beloved merely played the role expected of him, as he notes in "In All the Argosy of Your Bright Hair"—

> He saved me from my own hand
> And the five assassins nervous for the grandstand.
>
> My whole life in gratitude does him no good,
> Whose happiness was dancebands, beer, and baseball,
> Talked love to be polite.

—and is frigid emotionally: "Cold. Cold. Cold winds and colder heart" ("A Knight of Ghosts and Shadows").

All in all, the narrator comes to difficult conclusions about his beloved. He is simply one in a chain of many: "You were the first—but may not be the last / Contriver, O death-in-life long lover" ("Nor Mars His Sword"). He is misdirected, wasting his energy: "Sailor... // He is the hokum you have staked your life / On, breaking my heart, that cold mirror, with grief." He is never unique, but simply one of a herd: "What was the name of his ship? Did it matter? Sex / and the boredom of being together were always the same" ("Return of the Hero").

Thompson's narrator tries to make excuses for himself, for his inability to find love, by claiming "childlike the poet loves" ("This Life, This Death"), which suggests he's too trusting, too giving, too innocent to engage successfully in sexual relationships with the soldiers and sailors who give him their favors. Owen's narrator would not ever have made excuses, but then again, he would never have had to. Owen's narrator hid his true feelings—"love" and "lust"— behind "pity" and "sorrow," while Thompson put his—for better or for worse—on the line.

Whether military or, less often, civilian, Thompson's narrator's beloveds are always beautiful men. They are "tall sailors with yellow hair" ("Prothalamium for the Black Prince"). Their "eyes like islands lure the wanderer" ("Hyd,

Absolon, Thy Gilte Tresses Clere"). They are "sunlight boys" ("Field Music III"), each of whom is also a "pretty boy" ("Orphic Song"). "You were so many snapshot minutes," Thompson's narrator explains to his beloved, "such perfect / Photographs of fun" and "the fancy boy of heroes" ("Ocean Ode").

Just as often as being beautiful, they're dangerous simply because they're warriors on the prowl during a time of war. Each is, in his own way, a "butcher beast" ("Lament for the Sleepwalker")—another lovely play of words. Not only is his beloved a man of war, he's a "beast"—i.e., an animal full of hungers and the will to live—as well as a "butcher" who brings his "killer kisses" ("The Third Murderer") to their bed. He's not just masculine—i.e., *butch*—but extra-masculine: *butcher* than the typical, non-military man. His "regal muscles flex" ("Lament for the Sleepwalker") during love making. Feral, but for the taming uniform he wears and the barked orders he's obedient to, the narrator's beloved is the one who, "when death is not a metaphor / …dares to say love is like the war" ("The Loneliness for You Is Like the Wound") and to believe it.

Notes

i. Joseph Cady. "American Literature: Gay Male, 1900-1969," *Gay and Lesbian Literary Heritage*. Ed. Claude J. Summers. New York: Holt, 1995. 30-39.

ii. "'My Young Man of Mars': The Gay, World War II Love Poetry of Dunstan Thompson." *Value and Vision in American Literature: Literary Essays in Honor of Ray Lewis White*. Ed. Joseph Candido. Athens, OH: Ohio UP, 2000. 202-217.

iii. William Empson. *Seven Types of Ambiguity*. New York: New Directions, 1947.

"I Can Only Promise Poems": Finding Dunstan Thompson
by Katie Ford

Despite the fact that oceanographers refer to the eerie quiet and utter enormity of the deep sea as "the cathedral," they also suggest that perhaps living creatures emerged from the ocean and crawled onto land, becoming terrestrial millions of years ago, because the ocean was entirely dangerous. It's violent and dark, they say, far more violent than life on land. Imagine crawling out of the ocean to the relief of what, *only* by comparison, is a peaceful place to live.

There's a fight for life going on in every discipline, system, business, and art. Theologians, somewhat crassly, often refer to the major religions of our time as "historical winners." Christianity transformed overnight from a religion punishable by death to the state-sanctioned religion of the Emperor when Constantine converted in 313 A.D. That attachment to the Roman state—a state that used to send Christians to the lions—was crucial, if not definitive, in making Christianity an instance of one such "winner." What was heresy one night was orthodoxy by sunrise. Such labels come and go with time. It can be either confusing or liberating to watch thoughts and beliefs live and die because

Katie Ford holds advanced degrees in theology from the Harvard University Divinity School and creative writing from the University of Iowa. She is the author of two poetry collections: *Deposition* (Graywolf Press, 2002) and *Colosseum* (Graywolf Press, 2008). She is a professor of English at Franklin and Marshall College.

of these categories. But it's the way of history for certain writings to drift like filaments to the ocean floor while others—not always because they are superior or more astute—live on and on, surviving in a cathedral of thought.

Right now, in our own time, we have no idea which philosophies, religious movements, and poetries will last. Poets and novelists we adore might not be known in a hundred years. Cults and movements might rise into the mainstream and become institutions, or they might die off with their fifty-seven, or five hundred, or five million followers within a decade.

In modern poetry, for example, some work has just barely survived, and by no gentle path. Perhaps the most moving and somber of discoveries is the last poems of Miklós Radnóti, born in Budapest in 1909 and forced into labor camps during WWII. Shot when he could not continue to walk during a forced march, he was buried in a mass grave in Germany. His notebook of poems was exhumed along with his body. I've hardly ever read such transformative poems as those of Radnóti: "Will you write of me," a pilot asks the poet in Radnóti's "Second Eclogue." The poet answers, "If I live, if there's anyone left to read it." As a prisoner of war who became the prophet of his own death, Radnóti says, "Of all beasts man is the basest." We have the last poems of Radnóti because he carried them in the coat he was wearing when he was buried and later unearthed. His wife identified his remains by means of the poems in his pocket.

Part of our work as readers and writers, as citizens and artists, is to pass on the most human and humane, the most honest and stirring, the most clear-sighted and transcendent of what we've found in books, scholarship, and arts of all forms. Radnóti's buried poems are dramatic, unlikely discoveries. But there are quieter findings, findings that follow years of subtler losses. You likely haven't heard of Dunstan Thompson. I'm writing this essay to bring some of his lost poems to your collection of modernists.

Dunstan Thompson began writing in the time of T.S. Eliot, Wallace Stevens, Gertrude Stein, William Carlos Williams, Marianne Moore, E.E. Cummings, H.D., Ezra Pound, Robert Frost, Hart Crane, W.H. Auden, and the other giants of the Modern period. When has there ever been a fiercer ocean in American poetry? Even the giants I've named often got lost a bit in their own times: Stevens' *Harmonium*, for example, was sitting on remainder tables in 1923 once *The Waste Land* was released, which cast an epic shadow. In his autobiography, William Carlos Williams said *The Waste Land* "wiped out our world as if an atom bomb had been dropped upon it and our brave sallies into the unknown were turned to dust…. I knew at once that in certain ways I was most defeated." Poet and critic Randall Jarrell's writings were fundamental in arguing for the poetry of Williams, especially *Paterson*, during a time when Williams' reputation was not at all secured as a major poet. Jarrell later did the same for Elizabeth Bishop and Robert Lowell, who, of course, no one would consider "lost" these days. Behind many now-canonical poets was someone making a case for them.

Thompson, who lived from 1918-1975 and wrote with a war-broken, opulent lyricism, is nearly forgotten to us now. Philip Trower, who collected and saw to the publication of the posthumous collection, *Dunstan Thompson: Poems, 1950-1974*, and to whom Thompson dedicated his first two books, says that in the 1940s Thompson was not at all lost, but was a known and respected presence in American poetry. He was praised by Edith Sitwell and later remembered by Edward Field as "not far behind Hart Crane, Auden, Spender, Dylan Thomas as one of the stars of modern poetry." It's strange to hear such praise alongside a name that doesn't immediately bring to mind at least a few poems. Dunstan Thompson's poems, however, are not on our shelves.

It is Thompson's war poems that feel most necessary to me; these are the poems I want to recall as both a writer and reader. Thompson served in London as a GI in the Office of War Information for the American Army during WWII. Sometimes, the war drifts into his work as figuration or as shadow; elsewhere, it is all-consuming. What the war broke and took and left behind in him is what makes Thompson's most memorable poems astonishing. Even when the war is merely backdrop, it's the war poems that convince me I'm in the presence of the poet *feeling* something blank and haunted and human.

Here he is in just the beginning of "Circular Terror":

> After the drink, and after much too much
> To think about—the bills; unanswered letters
> From friends now fathom fived by war, who touch
> Like nerves a wound; and envy of my betters
> For poems I cannot write—after all this,
> I am persuaded by a second drink
> To try another bitch betrayal, kiss
> Goodbye my swimmer when he starts to sink.

"Kiss/ Goodbye my swimmer"—this high, elegiac sound and emotion strikes me, I think, because it's set against the roughened scene of drinking, bills, obligations, jealousy, temptation.... This is an all-American "list" poem, but what a list—among the mundane and petty worries, Thompson offers the stack of "unanswered letters" somewhere on a lonely desk. Unanswered, but not just that—these are letters from a friend who died in war before the poet has written back. Now the unanswered letters are not merely obligations but ghosts.

In the 1940s, the years of his early book publications, Thompson was a poet of sonnets, villanelles, patterned stanzaic verse (which he maintained throughout the years), dramatic monologues, faux-classical "Inscriptions," and traditional ballads. He writes with flourishes of rhyme and, at times, archaic contortions of syntax in service of that rhyme. Perhaps this is why the occasional "flat" sounds— sounds that feel basic, human, raw—are so startling. As I traced these stark lines through his work, I found that time and again these flattest sounds were in lines about war, lines that stand out like bare bulbs in the room of the poem, moments that interrogate the poet into his hardest honesty: the swimmer "starts to sink" Thompson says plainly, without any "poetic" turn of phrase, without any device save what's true in his imagination. The swimmer— the war-dead—sinks, and the flourish of "creativity" else- where calms down and stares the fact straight in the eye.

This plainspoken illumination happens also in one of the most powerful of Thompson's poems—it's an early poem, again, a sonnet called "This Loneliness for You is Like the Wound." Like all good sonnets, this one makes an argument. Like some sonnets, it ends in chastising its initial figuration as wrongheaded, inappropriate, even as a tres- pass against truth:

This loneliness for you is like the wound
That keeps the soldier patient in his bed,
Smiling to soothe the general on his round
Of visits to the somehow not yet dead;
Who, after he has pinned a cross above
The bullet-bearing heart, when told that his
Is one who held the hill, bends down to give
Folly a diffident embarrassed kiss.
But once that medaled moment passes, O,
Disaster, charging on the fever chart,
Wins the last battle, takes the heights, and he
Succumbs before his reinforcements start.
Yet now, when death is not a metaphor,
Who dares to say that love is like the war?

A poem that begins with loneliness becomes completely consumed by its stated likeness, a battlewound. As the poem unfolds, it shames its initial figuration into revision as the poet sees again the actual world of injury, army hospitals, the "bullet-bearing heart," the cots of waiting wounded, and the "fever chart." War does not leave Thompson with a set of equations, correlatives, or comparisons for his loneliness. Rather, it leaves him with the stark reality of the dying body, the realization that only *war* is like war. Love is not a war nor can it stand the test of comparison.

Part of the pain in this poem comes not only from the real death that occurs inside of it, but from the also-true fact that, at the end of this poem, loneliness remains, that it has not found its own articulation at all. The speaker must feel even lonelier than he did before the poem was first uttered. Nothing is like the violence of war, but after this realization, what is someone to do with the human loneliness that now seems small, even petty, in comparison?

Look at Thompson's vocabulary and syntax, how simplified it becomes after the acrobatics of description and figuration: "Death is not a metaphor," he says, while earlier his language twists and turns with such statements as "bends down to give/ folly a diffident, embarrassed kiss" and "he/ succumbs before his reinforcements start." The heavy truth hammers itself across the line, each word like a nail: DEATH IS NOT A METAPHOR. Not only is this poem insistent about the nature of love and death, it also identifies a "sin" common to poets—there are ways of writing poems, and ways of drawing comparisons that are so inappropriate they belittle the hard truth of life and death. They can sound, at times, harmless—"This loneliness for you is like the wound"—but they are not without harm, Thompson tells us. They harm our minds; they harm our ideas about human life.

Thompson doesn't need to tell himself twice that his loneliness ought never be equated with literal battle-wounds and death. The poem corrects this error in him, and elsewhere he cannot forget the war-wounded and the dead: The correction, perhaps, has gone too far. In fact, war is often so present in his mind that it won't let him locate himself physically once he is away from war:

Dazzled from the blazing, the bedazzling sea, he wonders where he is,
The stranger, the hero, the young man returning from the sundown war.
Others will tell him, he supposes, and already he can hear huzzas
Ring in the avenues, but lightly, lightly, as though women were
To welcome the armless, the cripples, the blind, and the laughing mad.
He is still whole, or seems so, and yet too often he thinks of the dead.
[from "Return of the Hero"]

The war poems, mostly printed in Thompson's second book, *Lament for the Sleepwalker* (1947), develop into an ethic of love; or, put another way, they meditate on questions of "love" and "not-love," as he does in "Songs of the Soldier":

These are no fictions but friends made
Mock of by heroics. The filth

Which washes them like unction should
Be for us as well. Soldier, that youth,
A drab death, might have grown great, had
He been you. To love him, tell the truth.
[from "Song of the Soldier"]

This is the task of the other war poems as well, including "The Everlasting Gunman," "This Tall Horseman, My Young Man of Mars," "Nor Mars His Sword," and "Dirge." The task of love, by means of poetry, is attended to earnestly in these poems. And, as Thompson says in "The Everlasting Gunman," "How shall I let you know these words have meaning/ Beyond the fakery, tricks of tongue you wonder/ At?" At times, a poet can feel that technique and craft applied to language renders it less true, an artifice of emotion. Thompson here wants to assure us that it is not the poem he is in service of, but love, meaning, and memory. He is right to have this concern. Craft without meaning is, indeed, like a intricately carved knife that won't cut.

When he was drafted into the United States Army in 1942, it was near the beginning of a fourteen-year period when Thompson had given up the intense Catholicism of his childhood and teenage years—not necessarily, Philip Trower says, because of any uncertainty regarding doctrine or belief, but because of what the religion forbade in daily life. It seems that it was not a crisis of faith that drove Thompson into a "lapsed" period of Catholic practice. Perhaps sexual and social, what was forbidden created a crisis of desire, not of belief. This is a crucial distinction because it provides a point of return to Catholicism for Thompson, a return that would occur in 1952. In other words, if he had fully doubted the theology and doctrine of his tradition, he wouldn't be likely to suddenly take it back up again years later. However, if he lapsed in *practice* but not in belief, then coming back to the Church later in life would not have presented theological and intellectual barriers, which are often insurmountable for those who have left the Church.

As I read poems from Thompson's collection *The Way Of Peace: Poems with Religious Themes* (included in *Dunstan Thompson: Poems 1950-1974*), written after his return to Catholicism, I sometimes sensed I was in the presence of something other than poetry, something that is not what I want when I read a poem. These later poems feel driven by Christian formularies and creeds, and when the poetry allows an institutionalized language to wash away the starkly singular discoveries elsewhere in his work, the poems begin to belong to the realm of the liturgical. Here the poems shift from poetry to liturgy—and Thompson seems not to fight against it at all. In this claim I mean two things: The language becomes formulaic and it seems meant to speak to and for a community of faith.

Liturgy, strictly speaking, is the set of linguistic formulas used to lead a religious body through a communal service. In the Catholicism Thompson practiced, worshippers learn and can expect the language of a service's invocation, absolution, Eucharist, creed, and benediction to be chanted or spoken at this week's service just as they were at last week's. Of course, there are sometimes various liturgies one church might choose from—Latin vs. English, for example, or the liturgy of matins vs. the liturgy of vespers—but the liturgical is meant, by repetition, to become a meditative, transformative, communal art of its own. Outwardly, its language is not meant to surprise; rather, the voices of many become the voice of one body reciting what's been recited for centuries. That, in part, is its power. And, of course, what happens to the worshipper internally is another mystery entirely. Surprise certainly occurs there, inside the body of the believer, but it is no longer seated in the language itself. Liturgy, in other words, relies on linguistic predictability that drives a community together while also evoking transformation in each believer.

Why, then, if liturgy has power, does it bother me so much when it enters a book of poems? It is largely the formulaic nature of liturgy that offends the heart of poetry. The poetic task is simply not the liturgical task, and when they are confused, when the liturgical is forced on the poetic, poetry suffers. It's lines are predictable, what the poem believes becomes rote and feels decided upon prior to the act of composition, whereas I believe strongly that the discovery a poem makes ought to come about *because of* the act of composition. We begin largely in the dark, discovering the right word as we go.

On the other side of things, imagine if a new poem were to be read as liturgy for a community of believers—

imagine a slightly obscure, intensely personal poem appearing as the morning's recitation. Not only would there be no sense of the historical there for the practitioner to attach to, there would be very little way for the recitation not to feel forced, foreign, and perhaps inappropriate to the occasion.

My argument against a large portion of Dunstan Thompson's religious poetry is also an argument *for* the other poems—and, as I've said above, the war poems in particular. It's also an argument against Thompson's own opinion that his first two books are not those that should be remembered. I will quickly trace through some lines of what I'll call "liturgical poetry" that I hope remind again how startling and original Thompson's war poems are. For example, in "Tenebrae," Thompson writes:

> Then from the darkness of the tower, birds
> Swoop, hopeful, towards the cross, alight along
> The outstretched arms, and rest.
>
> Perhaps the shadows have withdrawn a bit.
> Perhaps the cold is ebbing from my heart.
> Perhaps this could be peace.

And from Thompson's long poem, "Magdalen":

> High in the noonday sky,
> His arms thrown open wide,
> Love is about to die,
> With a thief on either side.

And, in "Rosalie," a tribute to his cat, Thompson writes,

> she plays so trustfully
> That I can see how we must be
> As small, as helpless, as in need
> Of all He has to give, so that,
> Dependent on His will, we plead
> Our littleness.

Probably the most heavily liturgical of the poems is "San Salvador," which has perhaps only one moment that breaks from Christian formulas of belief:

> Friend of the friendless, and the One who cares
> For every lonely, frightened, desperate man;
> Kind Heart, attentive to the feeblest prayers,
> Hastening to all who do the best they can;
> Dear Host, sole owner of the house He built,
> Who, coming unexpected to the door,
> Knocks, and, if answered, breaks the chain of guilt,
> And lets the soul go free to live once more;
> Shepherd, who seeks His torn and filthy sheep,
> Rejoicing when the longest lost is found;
> Father, who sees the broken wastrel creep
> Towards home, and, running, lifts him from the ground:
> This is our God, entreating us to prove
> His friends and live forever in His love.

It's the little "broken wastrel" that feels new to me, although it participates in the parable of the lost sheep. This is the Dunstan Thompson who largely borrows from, and is not fully engaged in, an act of creation, intentionally speaking to the masses to reiterate a truth that is far different from the truth Thompson speaks of when he says of those killed during the war, "To love him tell the truth."

Sometimes the war poem returns in the later work, but mostly I had to go back to the first two books to find it. Traveling back to the gorgeous and moving sequence, "Sonnets To My Father," from *Lament for the Sleepwalker*, I could hear again the flat, stark voice that indicates, in Thompson as in many other poets, a heightened state of illumination, however dire or lifeless that illumination might be:

> ... a war
> Broke your heart, as once before your son had.
> The years like roses darken, die: so fade

The roses on your grave. How the dead are
Easily put by. How the incomparable dead
Are easily forgotten. How still the dead.

Far more "religious," to me, is this sequence. Aren't these, too, confessions? *I broke my father's heart. I am liable to forget the dead.* This poem is not attached to religious ritual or liturgical formulas, but its existential questions and assertions are grounded in the same mind that seeks a religious life. And, as a meditative poem to his father, the personal starting point allows the poem to swell into its largest statements of all: The dead are still. The dead are easily forgotten.

"Again in All His Poor":
Dunstan Thompson's Incarnational Theology
by Jerry Harp

When Dunstan Thompson returned to Catholic faith
and practice in 1952, he was already undergoing the changes
in outlook leading toward what Philip Trower styles the "high
caliber and large quantity of religious verse in *The Red Book*"
(7). Many of the poems in this book, also known as *Poems
1950-1974,* emanate from a thoroughly incarnational theolo-
gy alive to the call for active engagement in the world. This
style of theology takes its cue from the doctrine that Christ
is God incarnate. The self-emptying—or kenosis—of the
divine in becoming human in turn also divinizes the created
world. Creation is pronounced good in the primal moments
of creation (Genesis 1), but it is further transformed by the
divine act of incarnation. An incarnational theology there-
fore sees in the created world opportunities for closer contact
with the creator. The seven sacraments of Catholic practice
are, in this theology, particularly intensive ritual moments that
open into encounters with the divine in all of the created
world, which is charged—as Father Hopkins wrote—"with
the grandeur of God" ("God's Grandeur"). In what follows
I shall explore some of the incarnational implications of a
selection of Thompson's later poems.

Jerry Harp's most recent book of poems is *Urban Flowers, Concrete Plains*
(Salt 2006). His study of cognition in the Renaissance, *"Constant
Motion": Ongian Hermeneutics and the Shifting Ground of Early Modern
Understanding,* was published by Hampton Press. His *"For Us, What
Music": On the Life and Poetry of Donald Justice* will be published by the
University of Iowa Press. He teaches at Lewis & Clark College.

The poem that is perhaps Thompson's simplest lyric—
consisting of no more than four lines and six words—
yields some complex implications about Jesus' salvific sub-
mission to crucifixion. Here is the whole of "On a
Crucifix":

> See
> Here at last
> Is
> Love.

The opening line, the single word "See," wavers between
the simple command form and a more colloquial, conver-
sational opening. It functions as both command and wel-
come, as it encourages attentiveness toward the crucifix
named in the title. The second line's "at last" accords with
the crucifix as the commemoration of a kind of ending,
Christ's humiliating and painful death by the Roman mode
of execution. At the same time, the line also accords with
Christ's death as the fulfillment of his salvific mission on
earth, the "at last" of what is accomplished. The poem's
first two lines, taken in isolation, call to mind one of the
seven final utterances of Christ from the cross: "It is fin-
ished" (John 19:30)—meaning both that his suffering is
complete and that what he has come to do has been done.
The moment ushers in a new era of history.

The line breaks isolating the word "Is" work, along
with the word "Here" in the second line, to place the com-
memorated action in the present time. Thus is disclosed
here a double emphasis of this very incarnational poem.
The action commemorated certainly takes place in the his-
torical past, but it is also an ongoing action whose work
and efficacy continue in the present day. For in the
Christian dispensation of belief—certainly the strain of it
articulated in this brief poem—all of human history is
redeemed and transformed by Christ's life, death, and res-

urrection. The redemption is an ongoing event that may be constantly experienced anew. The poem's final transformation of this humiliating form of death into an emblem of "Love" calls attention precisely to the transformative effects of Christ's life and death. The crucifixion becomes the chief symbol of divine self-emptying for the love of his creatures.

I take this poem also to be emblematic of Thompson's fundamental stance of faith, as is "Good Friday," which meditates on the day commemorative of Christ's crucifixion. Like "On a Crucifix," "Good Friday" is a deceptively simple poem whose complications emerge as one attends to its further implications. It begins as a fairly commonplace lament of lukewarm religious observance, as the speaker complains, "This day has lost its meaning," for it has become "just a day / On which to take the children / Somewhere else to play." Life goes on as usual, save for the inconvenience of having to go elsewhere to keep the children occupied. In the second stanza, however, the significance of the day is found inscribed in the very landscape: "The trees are not in leaf; / Gaunt arms are stretched out wide." Humans are meaning-making creatures, and reading the landscape within a framework of faith discloses a world that bears images of the love represented by the crucifix— the limbs of the bare trees become "Gaunt arms" stretched out like Christ's arms on the cross. As the poem laments an indifference to the iconographic possibilities of the landscape, it expresses sorrow over not only a failure of the faith, but also a failure of imagination; or it may even be that it laments a failure of faith that is also a failure of imagination, the ability to interpret all of the created world in relationship to one's vision and stance of faith.

The poem continues in a mode that could easily enough settle into a simple diatribe against the unobservant—the "girls in party dresses," those engaged in a "game of catch," the "motor-cyclist" headed to the beach—except that it makes a rather pointed turn to address a "you" whose circumstances emerge somewhat more fully than those of the previous, rather stereotyped figures:

> Your car—a chance for polish;
> The garden might be raked;
> And is not now the moment
> To see the rose-bush staked?

Poignant about this moment—save for the car, which keeps the scene firmly anchored in a contemporary scene—is the religious potential of the images. The garden needing to be raked may easily become the unweeded garden that once was Eden but is now the Garden of Gethsemani where Jesus weeps before his trial, agony, and death (Matthew 26:36-46; Mark 14:32-42; Luke 22:39-46). Likewise, the rose-bush calls to mind the rich array of imagery that has recurred through centuries of poetry, including the celestial ballet of the faithful in the form of a white rose in Canto 31 of Dante's *Paradiso,* as well as the fire and the rose that become one at the end of T. S. Eliot's *Four Quartets.* Within the context of the poem, these images' commonplace occurrence both alludes to their religious potential and calls attention to the missed opportunity for further significance.

The poem's eerie silence is one in which these further possibilities are left unarticulated:

> But strange this peace, this silence.
> A quietness seems to clash
> Against the world with violence.
> And some will still eat fish.

The quietness here is a not a contemplative silence, but rather a refusal of the meaning-making imagination that would read the world within the framework of faith. The poem calls attention to the violent refusal of a meaningfulness that could be made available by means of theological language and religious imagination and devotion, the latter of which is here reduced to the traditional Catholic practice of abstinence from meat on Fridays. Such a practice may have a deep and powerful meaning within a full framework of faith and practice; deprived of such a framework, however, it becomes mere banality.

A poem that pays tribute to a life of faith articulated in both imagination and action is the sonnet "Cardinal Manning," about the great 19th-century British Cardinal, one of the *Eminent Victorians* about whom Lytton Strachey wrote. Henry Edward Manning was born into quite favorable circumstances. His father was a wealthy merchant and a member of Parliament. Young Henry, early in life, had worldly ambitions of his own. Although these ambitions did not come to fruition, he found a place in the world as an Anglican priest. He became part of the religious phenomenon known as the Oxford Movement, which included Hurrel Froude, John Keble, and John Henry Newman. Eventually Manning, like Newman, found his way into the Roman Catholic fold, and later ascended to the position of Cardinal. According to V. A. McClelland's *Cardinal Manning: His Public Life and Influence 1865-1897,* which Philip Trower informs me Thompson had in his personal library (email 25 March 2009), Manning worked in many areas for social justice. He was a great promoter of education (including scientific education) and the labor movement. He exerted a direct influence on Pope Leo XIII's encyclical *Rerum Novarum* (1891), which called for recognition of a just wage as a basic human right, one that must not be left to the forces of the free market.

Thompson's sonnet calls attention to the tension between Manning's rather princely bearing and his devotion to social justice and the needs of the less fortunate:

> Prince, whom the people praised, though not the great
> Men, milling with their money-boxes through
> The palaces of chance and keeping state
> From slums that opened out their hearts to you…

As a Cardinal, Manning was indeed a "Prince of the Church," though he was a prince very much of and with the workers, not one enclosed in his palace. As Robert Gray recounts in his biography, while the Cardinal's clothes were threadbare, there was at the same time, in the words of Katharine Tynan, "an atmosphere of Royalty about him which might well be missing in the Courts of this world" (quoted in Gray 277). In Thompson's sonnet, the only palaces are the "palaces of chance," which I take to be the centers of monetary exchange, where the "great" go milling "with their money-boxes." The poem goes on to describe the rather stoic aspect that Manning presented in his later years; as Strachey wrote, by the time Manning was an old man, "his outward form had assumed that appearance of austere asceticism which is, perhaps, the only thing immediately suggested by his name to the ordinary Englishman" (112). The sonnet registers something of how this "appearance of austere asceticism" came to be:

> Your portrait shows you robed in God's own fire
>   Of love, skeleton of charity,
>   Whose eyes, too brilliant for their time, inspire
>   One most unlike you momentarily
>   To share the sight you, hungry, could endure:
>   Christ crucified again in all his poor.

This ascetic of God, with prophetic fury in his eyes—with their affinity to the "flashing eyes" of Coleridge's inspired poet, as to the "ancient, glittering eyes" of Yeats's men carved in Lapis Lazuli—inspire the vision of this poet to see Christ in the poor. It is in the suffering of the poor, the needy, the *anawim,* that the crucifixion happens again and again every day. This memorial to Cardinal Manning reminds us that in this crucifixion, as in that of Christ in his incarnation, there is something more than criminal. Such was Manning's devotion to and in engagement in a Gospel call to holiness in the world.

Thompson's "Fragment for Christmas," a prayer poem on the occasion of the day that most explicitly celebrates the incarnation, addresses the "Dear Lord" who was "rejected, tortured, torn" while "we were there." The poem's trans-historical terms recognize that because Christ died for all, including all sinners to come, all sinners were virtually present at the historical moment of the crucifixion. The prayer poem then ends with the speaker asking the Lord to "descend / Into each wrecked unstable house; be born / In us, a Child among Your former foes." The poem thus works in two historical directions at once; for just as the poem places "us" among the sinners at the crucifixion, so the incarnation becomes in the closing lines an ongoing event, continuing into the present moment. In the framework of this poem, Christ is here among us now, as he is "crucified again in all his poor" in the sonnet to Cardinal Manning. Both of these poems imply that all of human history is transformed, and continues to be transformed, by the events of Jesus' life, death, and resurrection.

Among Thompson's most powerful works bearing the stamp of his faith is his long poem "Magdalen," named for Mary Magdalen, who enters the gospels as a prostitute and ends as one of the first to bear witness to the resurrection event (see Matthew 28:1-10; Mark 16:1-20; Luke 24:1-12; John 20:1-18). Actually, each version of the resurrection narrative in the four canonical gospels names a different gathering of witnesses, though Mary Magdalen is the only constant in all four; in the Gospel of John, it is Mary alone who first goes to the empty tomb and finds the stone removed from the entrance. Thompson's poem begins with lines that establish a basic orientation to human nature, as well as to Mary Magdalene herself: "In the delightful cadence of her voice / The wickedness appeared a fragile thing." Is this "delightful cadence" a sign of her personality, or perhaps merely a tool in her livelihood as a worker in the "oldest profession"? Whatever the case, these lines imply that she is fundamentally good; whatever wickedness might be in her is fragile. This "wickedness" is made to "appear" in its fragility when she speaks; the quality of her voice makes this fragility apparent. Nevertheless, there remains something wild and marvelous in her speaking, for "when she spoke, her eyes, like desert fire, / Threw off the darkness of an old waste place." Something wild and potentially life-supporting—like fire in a desert place—lives within her yet. But her wickedness is not even so much a characteristic of Mary in herself as it is of what possesses her; the Gospel of Mark informs us that Jesus cast seven devils from her (16:9); Thompson takes up the image:

> Sometimes her looking-glass threw back a ray
> Of night light, and she saw the seven heads
> Behind her, each an angel from the wild
> Lost land of ruin—evil, avid, smart;
> Clever at doing over a child's heart.

She does not even get the dubious credit of what wickedness she carries, which has more to do with these smart and avid creatures, these fallen angels come in from the wilderness to haunt human civilization. Her heart retains something of a child's innocence.

The poem tracks the course of Mary Magdalen's development. Thompson's incarnational sensibility is such that he realizes we humans do not merely slough off earlier stages of our lives, but rather transform them in a constant process. As the poem points out, "Her odd distracting beauty bore the weight / Of years of jewels and youth grown desolate." And the speaker goes on to quote one who names her "Dear Mary, a leper at last." Named metaphorically a leper, she is the very image of the outsider who becomes a devoted insider, albeit in the rather renegade Jesus movement whose leader ends with the abjection of the cross, as the poem recounts in the rather jolting rhythms of its fifth section's ballad meter:

> High in the noonday sky,
>> His arms thrown open wide,
> Love is about to die,
>> With a thief on either side.

In the manner of the traditional Way of the Cross devotion, the poem meditates on who else is present at this scene of crucifixion, both literally within the narrative and virtually in relation to the concerns and choices that might place one there: religious officials, the soldiers dicing for the executed man's belongings, "mocking scholars," the victim's mother, along with his young apostle and friend John, as well as the Mary on whom this poem focuses— she "Whose sins have had their share / In blossoming that tree." This tree is the cross of execution, traditionally placed in opposition to the "tree of the knowledge of good and evil" (Genesis 2:9) from which Adam and Eve ate, bringing sin into the world. According to one configuration of images, the sins of humans nurtured this tree of sacrifice upon which Christ dies; in this way, the sins of all "have had their share / In blossoming that tree."

A crucial part of this poem's theology of redemption is not simply the juridical meaning of the cross as a sacrifice for the sake of fulfilling divine justice, but also its significance as an exemplary act that opens the human heart. If sin closes persons in on themselves, leading to our long history of selfishness and destruction, the way of the cross opens humans outward to others and the divine. Thus, Mary Magdalene "weeps / Outside her life." Her response to the crucifixion event already carries her outside herself and her life as she has known it so far. As the poem goes on to state, "His gift of sacrifice / Opens her rusted heart." The example of open-hearted and open-armed sacrifice has its immediate effect in opening this heart that had, through years of harsh experience, rusted closed. At the same time, the love that is life in Christ becomes a kind of art in the sense of a disciplined practice that strives, over a lifetime of devotion, to come as close as possible to perfection. Thus, the poem refers to love as "that suffering art." This is the art to which the poem pays tribute as it also pays tribute to Mary Magdalen herself:

> And so triumphant grief
>> Makes her the fourth to stay:
> Two innocents, a thief,
>> And a whore, together pray.

The ballad meter is often able to handle even the darkest subjects in an ironically lightsome manner that lends itself to rather complex tones (see Auden's "As I Walked Out One Evening"). This ballad section of Thompson's "Magdalen" is exemplary in this regard, as it doubles back to Mary Magdalen's earlier status—as "a whore"—while it also pays tribute to her steadfastness in standing by Jesus in his darkest moments. By identifying her in this way in a devotional context, he marks her pariah status even as she is on her way to becoming a saint. There remains in saintliness something renegade and outside the norm, as exemplified by the great saints (e.g., Francis of Assisi, Thomas More) through history who have stood as prophetic challenges to an easy status quo.

Thompson's version of the resurrection narrative, in which Mary Magdalen walks through the dawn to find

Jesus' tomb empty, recalls the scene in the gospels where the woman, conventionally identified as Mary Magdalen, anoints Jesus' body in preparation for his death:

The sun that shone beyond the morning star,
Dispersing night and coldness in the air,
Brought out the hidden birds, brought out the clear
Colour of the rose, brought out the more
Than aromatic fragrance of the myrrh
She carried through the dawn, and lit each tear
That mingled with the dew as she came near
The tomb in which the waiting angels were.

The explicit mention of the myrrh and "each tear" recalls that earlier moment of anointing (Mark 14:3-9; Matthew 26:6-12; John 12:1-8) in which the woman weeps on Jesus' feet and anoints his body in a deeply affectionate and even sensuous scene. Thompson's combination of Mary's devotion to Christ with this recollection of her sensuousness provides a vision of integration devoutly to be wished.

The poem shifts into a trans-historical mode that finds Mary Magdalen living, and preparing to die, in 20th-century France, where she participates in the Eucharist, which in Catholic tradition is the repetition in an unbloody manner of Christ's sacrifice on the cross:

So Calvary recurred:
And Christ in form of bread and wine
Offered his Body and His Blood for all the world
And for this woman who had loved him
Splendidly.

In her latter-day life in the 20th century, Mary receives in the sacramental elements of bread and wine the very Christ whose body she anointed centuries earlier.

When she herself dies and soars "along / The avenues of angels," she encounters others of her tradition, "all the holy other / Ancestral people": Adam, Eve, Abraham, David; but the poem's vision moves toward greater inclusiveness as this vision of final resurrection includes

> likewise all the lately
> Domiciled
> In greatly
> Separated centuries—
> Those from the smoke-charred caves
> And the imperial porcelain graves,
> From Nizhni Novgorod,
> From either Thebes,
> Palmyra, Cuzco, and Peking,
> Athens and Atlantic City...

This litany of place names from across the centuries converges into a vision of cosmic community, as these multitudes sing

> Among
> The Angels,
> Making up the number
> Of the rebels,
> Those who thought that they were wrecking
> Heaven...

Here Thompson takes up the same idea that Milton articulates in *Paradise Lost,* that humans compensate for the loss of the angels who fell with Satan. As the Father says to the Son in Book Seven of Milton's great poem:

> But lest his [Satan's] heart exalt him in the harm
> Already done to have dispeopled Heav'n
> (My damage fondly deemed) I can repair
> That detriment (if such it be to lose
> Self-lost) and in a moment will create
> Another world, out of one man a race
> Of men innumerable there to dwell,
> Not here, till by degrees of merit raised
> They open to themselves at length the way

Up hither, under long obedience tried,
And Earth be changed to Heav'n and Heav'n to Earth,
One Kingdom, joy and union without end. (150-61).

Thompson joins in the celebration of this full integration of Earth with Heaven and Heaven with Earth, in a Kingdom of "joy and union without end," as he articulates his own vision of the faithful in Heaven as their own brightness becomes part of the

> cataract
> Of light
> That pours about them as they praise
> God
> In the never-ending happy days
> That last...

As the poem comes to a close, Mary Magdalene is greeted by her namesake, the Blessed Mother of Jesus, and then by Jesus himself. In the final lines of the poem, the speaker himself addresses Mary directly as a saint, asking for her prayers:

> *Sancta Maria Magdalena,*
> *ora pro nobis.*
> Saint Mary Magdalen,
> pray for us.

In a final gesture of inclusiveness, the speaker makes the prayer first in the Catholic Church's traditional Latin and then in the vernacular. The form of the prayer is that of the litany of the saints, a mode of prayer that recognizes that the church community is inclusive of both the living and the dead. Now that Thompson is gone, the final poem of *The Red Book,* "Dedication," bespeaks also a community with the dead, as the poet continues to offer his work: "You have my poems, and they are yours, though mine."

Works Cited

Auden, W. H. *Collected Poems*. Ed. Edward Mendelson. New York: Vintage Books, 1976.

Coleridge, Samuel Taylor. *The Major Works*. Ed. H. J. Jackson. Oxford: Oxford University Press, 1985.

Eliot, T. S. *Collected Poems: 1909-1962*. New York: Harcourt, Brace & World, 1970.

Gray, Robert. *Cardinal Manning: A Biography*. London: Weidenfeld and Nicolson, 1985.

Hopkins, Gerard Manley. *The Poems of Gerard Manley Hopkins*. Fourth Edition. Ed. W. H. Gardner and N. H. MacKenzie. Oxford: Oxford University Press, 1967.

McClelland, Vincent Alan. *Cardinal Manning: His Public Life and Influence 1865-1897*. London: Oxford University Press, 1962.

Milton, John. *Paradise Lost*. Ed. Gordon Teskey. New York: W. W. Norton & Company, 2005.

Strachey, Lytton. *Eminent Victorians*. New York: Harcourt Brace Jovanovich, 1918.

Thompson, Dunstan. *Poems: 1950-1974*. Suffolk: The Paradigm Press, 1984.

Trower, Philip. "A Phoenix in a Desert: Dunstan Thompson." *Saint Austin Review*. (May / June 2008): 4-8.

Yeats, W. B. *The Collected Poems of W. B. Yeats*. Ed. Richard J. Finneran. New York: Macmillan Publishing Company, 1983.

A Phoenix in a Desert
by Philip Trower

A hundred or more years ago, when the method of analyzing ancient texts known as the "higher criticism" was at its height, it was fashionable for a time to maintain that Homer never existed.

His epics were attributed to a mob of minor Greek poets whose works had later been stitched together by a series of editors. Editors were then on the up and up. Since that time, thank goodness, sounder ideas have prevailed— at least in Homeric scholarship. Now it is generally agreed that Homer existed and was the author of the poems traditionally attributed to him so that today one can confidently assert that all the world's major poets, Homer included, have been known and acclaimed in their lifetime.

However, lower down the scale of poetic perfection or magnitude of production, there have occasionally been exceptions. In relatively recent times one thinks of Herrick and Gerard Manley Hopkins. Even Keats during his lifetime did not enjoy the status which, partly through the efforts of his admirer, the future Lord Houghton, he later came to occupy. And it is to this category of the late or slowly recognized that we must assign the American poet Dunstan Thompson.

For a short period, from the time he left Harvard in 1939 until the early 1950s, he enjoyed considerable acclaim,

---

Philip Trower is the literary executor of Dunstan Thompson. He is also the author of *Turmoil & Truth: The Historical Roots of the Modern Crisis in the Catholic Church* (Ignatius Press, 2003) and the historical novel *A Danger to the State* (Ignatius Press, 1998).

which explains the references to him in the New Catholic Encyclopedia under the heading "Catholic Poets". Poems by him will be found in many periodicals and anthologies of that period, particularly the successful anthologies of modern verse edited by Oscar Williams, and what the poet believed to be the best of these subsequently appeared in book form, which won him recognition as a young writer of exceptional talent in the literary worlds of both New York and London.

He became a figure in the London literary world during World War II while working there as a GI in the Office of War Information. In a letter to a friend, the poet Conrad Aiken gives us a glimpse of the impression he made. Aiken speaks of him as having "astounded Tom [T. S. Eliot] and everyone else in London by getting to know all the right people in two seconds flat. Which doesn't surprise me."

The "right people" meant the best known literati in the London of that time: the Sitwells, the Spenders, John Lehmann, Cyril Connolly. Eliot and Aiken he already knew. In two successive summers before the war (1938 and 1939) Thompson had spent a month studying writing and versification at a summer school which Aiken and his wife ran at Rye in England.

After the war came another year in New York. At that time, writes the poet Edward Field, "he was for my young self not far behind Hart Crane, Auden, Spender, Dylan Thomas as one of the stars of modern poetry." His first published volume, *Poems* (1943), had appeared to mostly highly favorable reviews while he was in Europe. The majority are very much war poems. The overriding subjects are love, death, friendship, the sorrow of partings, the joy of reunions, the paradoxes of army and wartime life in general. What among other things attracted attention were his poems' technical virtuosity, startling imagery, and arresting analogies.

There followed a six-month trip to the Middle East, recorded in a travel book, *The Phoenix in the Desert* and a second book of poems, *Lament for the Sleepwalker*, and two or three years later a novel, *The Dove with the Bough of Olive*.

Then what? An occasional poem appeared in the *New Yorker* or a literary periodical like Marguerite Caetani's *Botteghe Oscure*, culminating around 1955 in the publication by the *Paris Review* of a long meditation on the career and personality of T. S. Eliot after he received the Nobel Prize. Following that—as far as the world knew—nothing: a silence lasting for twenty years until his death in 1975 in the remote English village where he went to live in 1948, after his return from the Middle East, and which he never left again except for a trip to Rome in 1950 and an occasional visit to London or to friends elsewhere in the English countryside.

But the silence was not self-imposed. He continued to write prolifically until within a few weeks of his death and repeatedly submitted collections of these poems to American publishers through the late 1950s, 1960s, and early 1970s. The reasons for his lack of success, in spite of the efforts of friends in the New York publishing world who appreciated his poems' merit, are difficult to understand. Sudden shifts in public taste often are. But in this case it may, at least partly, have had something to do with his change of outlook and approach to poetry after he settled in England, a topic I will return to later.

The irony of the present state of affairs is that, in the opinion of many qualified people who have seen these later, mostly unpublished poems, they are, in their breadth of subject matter, variety of verse forms, and poetic power, greatly superior to the two early books which got him a name. And it is surely no less ironical that it is these later poems, written subsequently to 1950, which he hoped to be remembered by, while he gave instructions that the two early books were not to be reprinted.

After his death, five hundred copies of the later poems were privately printed and the fact that each is a volume of 361 pages gives some idea of the scale of his output. In order to distinguish this collection from the two earlier, commercially published books of poems, I will for the rest of this article refer to it as *The Red Book*. *The Red Book* is really three separate books of poems arranged by the poet himself, with a short section of additional poems found in drawers and folders after his death. A few copies of *The Red Book* are in libraries, the majority of the rest in private hands. It is largely on this little flotilla of paper glue and buckram that his literary survival depends. There remain about 140 unsold copies which, as the poet's executor, I have donated to the *St. Austin Review*, and from which they will be available to anyone interested. That they are a literary curiosity of very great interest seems to me unquestionable. But I believe they will one day be valued for far, far more than that.

Reviewing the book in the *Hillsdale Review* (vol. 8, no. 3) some years ago, Gregory Wolfe, after describing Thompson as "a lyric poet of great versatility and depth," goes on to say: "in my opinion, Thompson is easily one of the finest twentieth-century poets of a Christian—and specifically Catholic—sensibility." He quotes as an example of his exceptional lyric gift the poem "Passage" (340). Four other poems from *The Red Book* can also be found in *Flowers of Heaven*, the anthology of Christian verse recently compiled by *StAR*'s editor.

At this point, some paragraphs about the poet's personality and background will perhaps help to throw light on what I think makes this body of verse special and different from that of some of his more successful contemporaries.

Although he loved his country dearly, neither by temperament nor upbringing was he mainstream American. There was nothing un-American, of course, in his having been highly intelligent, witty, imaginative, or, when what he saw as truth was at issue, morally courageous to an exceptional degree. But at the same time, he was nervous and highly strung, physically far from robust and for the most part almost comically impractical. Organizing daily life finally became such a major obstacle to tranquility and peace of mind that towards the end of his New York days he gave up trying to cope with an apartment and lived in the Algonquin Hotel. This had another advantage. He could not bear being alone. In a hotel lounge he could sit contentedly, reading for hours at a time as long as there were other people around.

Reading and conversation were not only his greatest enjoyments. One could describe them as occupations. Indeed, along with thinking and writing, they account for the greater part of the time allotted him in this world. But unexpectedly, as far as reading goes, his interests were for the most part non-literary. He seldom read novels or anything resembling what used to be called *belles lettres*. Even poetry, or at least other people's poetry, he gave up reading towards the end of his life.

History was his great love, particularly the history of the ancient world. But history also included current affairs. His appetite for newspapers and periodicals of every kind was almost an addiction. It was as though he couldn't know enough about the mysteries, follies, beauties, terrors, and dramas of human existence, which throughout his life both fascinated and amazed him. All this fed his poetic imagination in a very special way, as readers of *The Red Book* will discover. I can think of no other large body of verse in which so many of the poems have historical personalities or episodes as their subject matter or evoke so successfully the ethos of past epochs. An example of the latter would be the long meditation "Edwardian Seascape with Figures," about a once-fashionable English seaside resort on the eve of World War I and its state of decay after World War II; and of the former the large number of epigrammatic quatrains summing up the careers, vices, and virtues of historical figures, many of them, in my opinion, worthy of Belloc. Here, for instance, is one on the Roman Emperor Augustus:

> The grace is Greek, the risky stance superb
> As, like a charioteer, he bends to curb
> Rome and the Senate with a sparkling threat;
> Then rounds the circus without one upset.

Also unusual is his use of the sonnet for humorous as well as serious purposes, exemplified in the poem "Tradition."

To his gifts as a conversationalist all who knew him have borne witness and, as is usual in such cases, what they remember best, especially those who knew him in early manhood, is how much he made them laugh.

But there was more to it than that. From the start, he was never just a clever young man "with a gift of the gab," as Aiken noted. Under the sparkling surface there were depths which owed their origin in part to that profound sense that nothing lasts or ultimately quite lives up to its reputation, which the ancients expressed in the words *eheu fugaces* and *sunt lacrimae rerum*, and which dominates the Book of Ecclesiastes. At present it is highly unfashionable, which may partly be what eventually turned the publishers' readers against him. Yet in a sense it ought surely to be a component of every truly poetic and still more every Christian mind, provided it is balanced by faith, hope, and charity.

An incident in the 1920s will give some idea how deep it lay in the present case. The future poet was about ten and on holiday with his parents in France, where they one day visited Versailles. After seeing the whole works—the palace, the private apartments, the gardens, the two Trianons, the

Hameau—the little boy looked up at his parents with a perplexed look and said quite seriously, "Is that all?"

Behind or beneath these characteristics lay a deeply, and in a certain sense exceptionally, Catholic childhood. Of his parents he used to say that they would both have died for the Faith but would have mounted the scaffold from opposite sides. This was his way of describing their different religious backgrounds.

The father, Terry Brewster Thompson, a naval officer and son of New England convert parents, had been brought up and educated in France where his father was head of the Associated Press. The result of this mixture of influences, French and New England Puritan, was what his son described as an "almost Cistercian religious austerity."

In contrast, he would describe his mother's devotional life as "Italian and baroque," and this was what initially prevailed in his own spiritual formation. She, on her mother's side, came from an old Maryland Catholic family related to the Carrols and Lees—the poet was proud of being descended from Daniel Carrol of Carroltown, the only Catholic Founding Father, and of being a cousin of the famous General Lee of Civil War fame—and on her father's side from Louisiana Catholics with strong French links.

Because of this, from the time he was a small boy, he was used not only to a cosmopolitan family atmosphere, but to meeting the higher clergy of the Washington-Baltimore area, kissing the rings of cardinals and archbishops, serving their Masses, hearing higher ecclesiastical chitchat, and taking part in frequent religious ceremonies. Before he was twelve he had been three times to Europe and Rome, where he was present at the canonisations of St. Joan of Arc and St. Theresa of the Child Jesus, and of course met the reigning pope, Pius XI. From the age of seven he served the daily early morning Masses of the

Redemptorist father at Annapolis when his father was teaching at the Naval Academy there.

Today there are people who would regard such a childhood as a "religious hothouse" or positively "unnatural". But he seems to have absorbed it as naturally and without damage as another boy would have being taken constantly to football and ice hockey matches. It did not prevent him from enjoying the company of other children or being popular at school. The natural and supernatural orders were intertwined in a way that made them a single whole, of which one day being a priest seemed a more or less inevitable part. He did not, of course, become a priest. But eventually, after intervening disasters, this total immersion in the traditional practices of centuries of Catholic life and culture accounts in large part, I believe, for his having died a Catholic.

However, even stronger than his mother's influence on his life and outlook was eventually to be that of his great-aunt Mrs. Edward White, wife of the first Catholic Chief Justice of the United States. The Whites were childless and regarded the poet's mother as a surrogate daughter. Because of this, and because his father was often at sea, the poet spent a large part of his boyhood at her house in Washington next to what is now St. Matthew's Cathedral, with holidays in the summer at the house she took every year in New London.

The short lyric "Summertime" captures some of the intoxication he felt on the yearly journey northward to Connecticut:

> Suddenly the sea was there
> Sparkling like a different life
> Deep blue and white—
> A small boy watching while the Pullman swayed
> Close to where the waters were so dashingly arrayed.

Surely, the first look
Of Heaven
Will be like the sea at Saybrook.

Aunt Leita, as she was called, was a major influence on his life in two respects. She provided him with an experience of stability, security, ordered love, and predictability which came in retrospect to seem like a foretaste of heaven, and when she died she left him enough money to live on for the rest of his life without having to take a job. It was not riches. But it was enough to keep him afloat in reasonable comfort provided he handled it wisely. That was in 1936. The poet was sixteen, and there were no doubt members of his family who predicted that giving a young man financial independence so early in life must certainly lead to disaster. And at first they would have seemed to be justified. Yet as things turned out, Aunt Leita proved right. Given his impracticality, it was his independent means which kept him afloat until God came to the rescue.

Rescue became necessary because some time between his final year at a Catholic prep-school in Connecticut and his first year at Harvard he lost his faith and adopted what was eventually to be a highly promiscuous homosexual lifestyle.

The years after Harvard were the years of his public success as a poet and writer. But by 1948, throwing off the Faith was proving not to be the intoxicating access to freedom and happiness which it had seemed to promise at first, as can be seen in the small number of poems from this epoch with a Baudelairean sense of desolation. The sonnet (299) beginning "In rain, in loneliness, the late despair" perhaps best describes the desolation, while the "Poem" (351), in which "Eros, his plumes bedraggled by the snow / came on me walking in the frozen park," conveys the chilling experience of an encounter with total lovelessness:

> But there was light enough to see his face,
> Those eyes of ice, that mouth impassioned stone,
> The whole expressionless, as though a place
> Where happiness and suffering were not known.

Here, by contrast, in the poem "Fragment from Christmas," is the situation twenty years later.

> Dear Lord, and only ever faithful friend,
> For love of us rejected, tortured, torn—
> And we were there; who on the third day rose
> Again and still looks after us; descend
> Into each wrecked unstable house; be born
> In us, a Child among Your former foes.

But this is not the place for the story of his return to the practice of his religion, which took place in 1952, and which needs an article to itself. Here I am concerned with him chiefly as a poet, about which I will make one final point.

Although his return to the Church and the Faith did inevitably change his outlook in significant ways and is responsible for the high caliber and large quantity of religious verse in *The Red Book*, a change of content of a different kind and still more of style and technique had already begun as far back as 1945.

With regard to the content, there is an enormous broadening of subject matter which makes reading *The Red Book* like a journey of adventure through a new country, in addition to being, what is more usual on taking up the work of a new poet—an encounter with a fresh poetic sensibility.

As for style, what is chiefly remarkable, I think, is the vast variety of verse forms it incorporates, old as well as new. The early poems, in spite of their technical originality, have a certain uniformity of style in the sense that almost all bear the stamp of the poetic "modernism" which, from the 1920s, reigned almost unchallenged for the rest of the century. This does not mean that in the later poems Thompson rejects the positive acquisitions of poetic modernism; I am referring to its greater use of free verse and its abandonment of a special kind of diction, subject matter, and sentiment considered as being alone appropriate for good poetry. But one could speak of a return to the "grand tradition" and an opening of it up to the benefits of poetic modernism while leaving behind that movement's defects as passing peculiarities of a bygone age.

In a recent article on the English poet John Heath Stubbs, a contemporary of Thompson's, the English author and critic A. N. Wilson spoke of Heath Stubbs as having done something similar. If this is true, both poets, I suggest, deserve a long and loud salute. But for that actually to happen in Thompson's case, the contents of *The Red Book* will first have to become as widely known as I believe they deserve to be.